STORY ABOUT FEELING

Look how they fly...
Alright. I'll make camp there under.

Magpie Geese - *Ian Morris.*

STORY ABOUT FEELING

Bill Neidjie

edited by

Keith Taylor

Magabala  Books

Acknowledgements

Grateful thanks to the artists of Oenpelli, Maningrida, Goulburn and Elcho Islands. All artists or their descendants were approached for permission to use their works. Thanks to Margie West and the Northern Territory Museum of Arts and Science, to Michael O'Ferrall and the Art Gallery of Western Australia, for guidance in the use of original bark paintings. Special thanks to Joy Maddison for her encouragement throughout and to Jeremy Russell-Smith for his assistance with early editing.

First published by Magabala Books as a project of the Kimberley Aboriginal Law and Culture Centre, 1989
Reprinted by Magabala Books Aboriginal Corporation in 1993, 1996, 1998, 2002
2/15 Saville Street, PO Box 668, Broome, Western Australia 6725
Email: info@magabala.com
Website: www.magabala.com

Magabala Books receives financial assistance from the Commonwealth Government through the Australia Council, its arts funding and advisory body, and the Aboriginal and Torres Strait Islander Commission. The State of Western Australia has made an investment in this project through ArtsWA in association with the Lotteries Commission.

Editor/design Peter Bibby
Front cover – John Frost, *Knowing My Past*
Back cover – Traditional figures, unknown artist
Inside front cover – Brian Stevenson *Jabiru*

Typeset in Helvetica
Printed by Frank Daniels, Perth

National Library of Australia Catalogue-in-Publication data:
Neidjie, Bill, 1913-
Story about feeling

ISBN 0 9588101 0 9
I. Taylor, Keith, 1954-. II. Title
A821.3

Preface

Story About Feeling is the name Bill gave to the talks we had together in October and November of 1982. I recorded many hours of Bill's words on audio tape during that time. This work is a transcript from those tapes.

The original has been edited down and arranged into themes, under chapter headings. Various elements of a theme are highlighted in a story-list at the beginning of each chapter. A full story-list appears at the end of the book, as a reference guide.

I haven't attempted to explain or interpret Bill's story. As he says, "Someone can't tell you. Story e telling you yourself." His use of this language is not standard English, so a glossary of terms can be found on pp. 176-7, to assist the reader when necessary. Places referred to in the text are shown in the maps on pp. 172-175.

* * *

In a world where our vision becomes ever more blinkered by the dominance of a single cultural way and where such dominance threatens the survival of other ways of thinking and being, there is an urgent need for more stories like this. I trust that the reader will enjoy it as much as I have enjoyed preparing Story About Feeling, and as much as Bill Neidjie forever enjoys telling it.

Keith Taylor

if you got story, heart...
then speak yourself, stand for it!

Bill Neidjie - *Ian Morris.*

A Brief Biography

Bill Neidjie was born at Alawanydajawany along the East Alligator River sometime betweeen 1911 and 1913. He spent most of his childhood in his father's country, Bunitj Clan land, on the western side of that river. Bill talks of attending school at Oenpelli Mission for two years around 1927. When his father died in 1928 Bill followed his mother to Coopers Creek where they camped for about four years, living on bush-tucker.

Before the war Bill had a variety of jobs which usually paid no money but provided tea, sugar, meat, flour and tobacco. He worked for eight years at timber-mill camps, shifting every two years as the timber ran out. Bill talks of four such camps: Mt Norris, Buffalo Creek and two around the Van Diemen Gulf.

He spent a little time in Darwin before the war cleaning houses and cutting grass for people and talks of there not being many houses in Darwin at that time and of today's suburbs of Rapid Creek and Nightcliff being all bush and jungle.

During the war Bill earned his tucker and tobacco by hunting turtle and providing firewood for Col. Bill Sanderson of the Australian Airforce whose job was to keep the lighthouse at Cape Don. Along with other Aboriginal men, Bill used to chop mangrove wood, float it in a line down to the jetty and load it onto a trolley, which they would push over a kilometre to the three houses that needed the wood. Each household would pay Bill and his friends a bag of flour for their toils.

Both before and after the war, Bill worked for Leo Hickey on his lugger along the north coast for close on 30 years loading and unloading supplies. He is a tall strong man and it may have been during his time with Leo that he earned the name of 'Big Bill Neidjie'. Stories tell of Bill unloading large sacks of flour from the lugger, one sack on each of his shoulders.

At Bagot, in Darwin, Bill grew a magnificent vegetable garden. Then in 1979 he returned to take up permanent residence on his Bunitj Clan land and has devoted much of his time since then trying to ensure that his knowledge and love of the country will not be lost but can be shared by us all.

K.T.

Corroboree - Oenpelli 1968.

Eagle there!
e can look plain and water there longside

and you feel yourself   Kakadu - *Ian Morris.*

CONTENTS

Oenpelli 1967.

LAYING DOWN

This story e can listen careful
and how you want to feel on your feeling.
This story e coming through your body
e go right down foot and head
fingernail and blood... through the heart
and e can feel it because e'll come right through

1

Camp at night seen from above - the Milky Way, ashes of campfires, two bark huts and sleeping families - Oenpelli 1968.

Well I'll tell you about this story,
about story where you feel...laying down.

Tree, grass, star...
because star and tree working with you.
We got blood pressure
but same thing...spirit on your body,
but e working with you.
Even nice wind e blow...having a sleep...
because that spirit e with you.

Listen carefully this, you can hear me.
I'm telling you because earth just like mother
and father or brother of you.
That tree same thing.
Your body, my body I suppose,
I'm same as you...anyone.
Tree working when you sleeping and dream.

This story e can listen carefully, e can listen slow.
If you in city well I suppose lot of houses,
you can't hardly look this star
but might be one night you look.
Have a look star because that's the feeling.
String, blood...through your body.

That star e working there...see?
E working. I can see.
Some of them small, you can't hardly see.
Always at night, if you lie down...
look careful, e working...see?
When you sleep...blood e pumping.

So you look...e go pink, e come white.
See im work? E work.
In the night you dream, lay down,
that star e working for you.
Tree...grass...

I love it tree because e love me too.
E watching me same as you
tree e working with your body, my body,
e working with us.
While you sleep e working.
Daylight, when you walking around, e work too.

That tree, grass...that all like our father.
Dirt, earth, I sleep with this earth.
Grass...just like your brother.
In my blood in my arm this grass.
This dirt for us because we'll be dead,
we'll be going this earth.
This the story now.

Stone e never move
Rock e don't move round,
e got to stay for ever and ever.

E'll be there million, million...star.
Because e stay, e never move.
Tree e follow you'n'me,
e'll be dead behind us but next one e'll come.
Same people. Aborigine same.
We'll be dead but next one, kid, e'll be born.
Same this tree.

Star e'll stay for ever and ever.

Freshwater crocodile - *Bijinyarra*, Maningrida 1967.

When you laying down in the night, look that star.
I was. I look star.
I remember back when I was young.

That three there...   *
That's the one crocodile!

That crocodile e float there and e look.
 E said...
        "I'll get im that middle one."

Canoe...stringybark canoe.
E watching that middle man there,
sitting down middle, feeling sick...
        "I'll get im, kill im that middle one!"

So that bark, that canoe, e tip over.
E got that man in the middle because e was sick.

See right hand side; three again there?
That crocodile e's got im now.
So e bright-up little bit more.

* in the Orion constellation.

They used to tell us...

> *"Look that moon, middle of it...*
> *that man and dog!*
> *Good eye...*
> *you can look one dog, one man up there.*
> *That's the story for you so e can look.*
> *If not...*
> *well e can look that man when you sleep.*
> *You dream."*

"Yes...I can see little bit black there.
Yes, dog and man, arm with spear,
walking and dog behind."

> *"When you go hunting you want dog.*
> *Well that's the dream over there."*

Kangaroo and dingo - *Mangudja,* Oenpelli 1967.

"Nagakeetch" spirit man hunting a kangaroo - Oenpelli 1971.

One dog and one man you can look.
Slow you can look.
Because that man e had own spear, own womerra,
I think fire-stick and might be goose-wing.

You can't hardly see goose-wing now
because people this time...matches!
Before...they put goose-wing there. *
You know, might be in the wet **
you got to cook fire so e burn quick.
You cook anything and come back home.

Old people I said...
    "Why you carry wing?"
    "Because that story up there; have a look!"

They used to lay down...look that moon.

* Forewing of a goose used as a fan to make draft in wet conditions.

** The wet-season of heavy monsoonal rains.

Moon. Moon is man. E said...
    "People...they'll come back,
    like I'm doing."

And Native-cat, e said...
    "No!
    We'll do other way.
    We can dead*...never come back!"

So everyone they jump up.
They was burning him,
burning him with fire nearly killing him.
So e got every spot!

Moon make good.
He said, "Well they'll come back alive."
So e can look moon is finished
but e still come back.
We...we'll come to earth,
we'll be like earth.

* Can die, be mortal.

The double men Barun-Barun who made
the large spearheads - unknown artist, Oenpelli 1948.

E can see moon because e's changing it.
E go dark but e come back new...you got light.
Close on west side e can see new moon.
E go middle of the year, top,
middle night...e go middle age.
E go low...e getting little bit old now,
grey hair like me.
E go that moon just about daylight
and e comes out half-way...
e feeling sick.
E say...
        "Well I nearly finished!"

E getting old now,
right down with a walking stick.
Next morning, early, you can't see...
that mean e's finished.

That's the one e come back...
        "New moon!"

E come back like young,
just like baby when they born.

E not moon but man himself.
So e turn...e went up there.
E dead but e come back.
We spoil it...
That Native-cat...
no-good, silly man!

Because they used to tell im story like that.
I never see im now...bit rough.
You stand there and quiet everybody.
They used to tell me...

>*"That's true story, now you got to keep it.*
>*If someone e got to ask you, you tell im.*
>*No-matter fifty, two hundred,*
>*they'll listen to you.*
>*Stand middle and tell.*
>
>*E go might be thousand million,*
>*million, million year.*
>*E can't wear out...moon.*
>
>*Star...about million, million year,*
>*e'll still be there.*
>
>*We...we gone*
>*but youngest they come."*

Because all that story up there
and here, all this dream here,
that's the one up there.
Star up there but here e made something...
rock or billabong or might be river.
That way star there.

I can touch if e close...but too far, e can see.
E can have a look nice lovely night,
all clear without cloud...but that for us.
Earth and star, sky, cloud, tree, animal...

10

The morning stars, Garakma, which appear during October. The large star is the man Garakma, the smaller star his wife, circles with dots are girls, star designs are the boys of the family
- unknown artist, Oenpelli 1948.

I can listen over there flying-fox.
Coming out in the night eating his dinner or supper.
E looking for in the night, e allowed in the night
looking for something to eat.
E can't come daytime because im very shy.

In dream e made that womerra.
That way you see his claw-foot
hanging down other way.
Because that spirit for us . . . same as im.
E was man but we call im Gulluban...
that flying-fox now.

That flower we call im Warrgarr, that his feed.
E eating his food in the night till daylight.
Just about daylight e not there
because e'll have to give im chance now honey-bees.

Bush-honey-bees e go get that flower.
Each flower e get half, half.
E make wax and we get honey then,
nice clean honey.
So that way flying-fox e work.

When you in 'business' you can't touch flying-fox.
You can't eat when you young.
They used to tell us...
        "Don't eat that!"

Even water-python, grey one.
We never eat that.
But all, each animal got 'business'.
They got story each.

Bumabbuma, orange horseshoe bat and Djilawarnbed possibly a small
banded snake, found among leaf litter in caves favoured by the bat.
Bumabbuma was a man before he changed to his present form.
He killed a cannibal spirit, Murul, who travelled from the West 'killing
everyone as he came' - *Bunkaniyal*, Maningrida 1979.

That white-chest eagle,
that's the one we say e can go billabong,
e can go salt-water
but that proper big one...black one!
E can go dry land and rock country.

All black. Sometimes little bit spot, yellow
but proper black one.
E can kill im black wallaby,
Black kangaroo that eagle can kill im.

We brought up like all the animal and bird
because eagle e fly round or might be jabiru,
might be brolga, might be goose.

Goose good eating. You got to eat goose
because goose e breed up again.
Soon as wet, e got to make egg...good eating.
Or goanna or long-neck turtle...
brought up because for us to eat.

Long-neck turtle you got to eat
but e get plenty again, e breed up more.
Even goanna e'll breed again.
Geese...e can eat two-hundred but e'll come.
E breed up here, egg...
another plain, another plain, another plain.
You might get one thousand and thousand goose.

Crow...e was eating this rubbish.
So e said...
"Go on, get out!"

E man alright.
That hawk, all them...men
but they went* to all the bird, animal.
Any animal...we came from this world with the story.
You know, e had story with us.

Animal they come out in the night...insect
because e made up.
Some insect daytime but most in the night.
Some bird, I think owl,
e looking for something to eat in the night,
daytime you can't mostly look im.

Eagle hide in the tree or might be rock,
little bit of shelter where nobody can go,
quiet and having a sleep.
If somebody there, e listen, e go other place.
Any animal e change it place
because e might listen noise...
e don't like it.

But all that animal for this world.
Same us people.

* They turned into their animal forms.

Wind for us.
That way e come blow wind
and you feel it lovely, nice,
feel it cold now...lovely.
And I love it that wind.

That wind is wind for anybody...no-matter who.
Sometimes when you feeling you like outside
you might say...
>"I camp out there, camp outside
>and I might go sleep."

I like im.
I like im camp outside
because of course you got to sleep outside,
you got to feel im that wind and look star!

And that wind e blow, blow, blow, blow
and e can listen leaf
and you feeling yourself,
your body yourself,
you feeling...
>"Ahh...good sleep! I'll listen that wind."

Because e talking to you I suppose.
You go sleep. E say...
>"Well you might good sleep."

I feel it that wind, e coming slow...there!

Sometimes strong wind e blow strong, strong...
Some they might say...
      "What for e blow strong wind?"

Because e blow wind
because e's yours.
Not for yours yourself...
for anybody.

You feel it no wind...hot!
You'll be looking for wind,
no-matter this time fan they make im.

People used to camp...but hot!
      "Hey! Where this wind?
      Where this wind gone?"

That's why I'm outside.
Last night...oh, e blow wind.
Yes...
that's the one for anybody.

Mankolk, cocky apple, bears a pulpy and sweet fruit
in the late dry season, while only a small shrub and
later as a medium sized tree - *Bunkaniyal,* Maningrida 1979.

That tree now, feeling...
e blow...
sit quiet, you speaking...
that tree now e speak...
that wind e blow...
e can listen.

Eagle there!
It's alright...
e make you "oh"
and look across there,
e can look plain and water there longside
and you feel yourself
how your body.

We think.
Story we think about, yes.
Tree...yes.
That story e listen.
Story...you'n'me same.
Grass im listen.
You'n'me same...anykind.
Bird e listen...anykind, eagle.
E sit down. E want to speak eagle eh?
Im listen. You listen...eagle.
Because e put im through your feeling.
But for us eagle...
all same.

Listen carefully, careful
and this spirit e come in your feeling
and you will feel it...anyone that.
I feel it...my body same as you.
I telling you this because the land for us,
never change round, never change.
Places for us, earth for us,
star, moon, tree, animal,
no-matter what sort of a animal, bird or snake...
all that animal same like us. Our friend that.

This story e can listen careful
and how you want to feel on your feeling.
This story e coming through you body,
e go right down foot and head, fingernail and blood...
through the heart.
And e can feel it because e'll come right through.
And when you sleep you might dream something.

You might dream moon,
or you might dream water, storm.
You might dream tree, wind...

Oh anything e can dream...that dream e's true.
You having a sleep
but your spirit over there where you dream.
Daylight...e come back.

Now I telling story I can listen this.
You listen that wind e come more.
Tree e start moving round and feeling.

Djorrkkundedjmildurngh. This fig survives almost on bare rock.
Its name means 'possum eat tree' - a food of Djorrrkkun, the rock
ring-tail possum - *Bunkaniyal,* Maningrida 1979.

TREE

I drive
I see big lumber-log lying down
That way you get pain in your back
You know, that tree e push
Bulldozer e pull it out big roots
That one e cut your back
E should be stay in ground for us
This tree for us.

22	Because you want road this time
23	That leaf e pumping
24	Don't be rough
28	Fire is nothing
29	White-ants!
30	Bulldozer e killing it
33	Shade
34	Good smooth tree
36	That signal

We got tree here one...
    "Might be in the road..."

Because you want road this time I suppose.
Before...walk around that tree and walk along.
Wasn't any grader-hole anywhere.
This time...big truck, gravel truck...

So bit bent...in the road there they said...
    "Well you touching it there."

So I said...
    "Well you must knock im down."

I didn't say...
    "You might feel it..."

I said...
    "E's alright, doesn't matter
    because we need that road."

Earth...exactly like your father or brother or mother
because you got to go to earth,
you got to be come to earth,
your bone...because your blood in this earth here.

Tree same thing. E watching you.
You look tree you say...
    "Oh!"

That tree e listen to you, what you!
E got no finger, e can't speak
but that leaf e pumping his.
Way e grow in the night while you sleeping...
you dream something,
that tree and grass same thing...
e grow with your body, your feeling.
When you sleep, good sleep in the night, I ask you...
    "Good sleep?"
    "Yes!"

Well tree e same way, e worked with you.
When you feeling tree e work with you tree.
You cut im little bit, you got water coming out.
That's his blood, same as your blood. So e alive.

Well you can feel im there arm...
doctor e feel im there...
well that tree same as you.
If you feel sore...
    "Oh, I'm my body sore!"

Well that mean somebody killing tree
because your body on that tree or earth.

Well they told me...
    "Don't be rough!
    If you too rough...
    little bit of mistake."

I said...
    "What this...'little bit of mistake'?"
    "Something...
    You never tell on your body?"

I said...
    "Why?
    I can tell my body...
    no-one can kill me with spear!"
    "We know no-one can kill you 'outside'
    but when you feeling, feeling on your body
    what e coming in on your feeling...
    something e'll come...
    you get headache...is nothing
    but when you get very bad sick..."

I said...
    "Why?"
    "Well I'll tell you...see that tree?"

"Yes...
I chop it down that big tree.
I play...I cut it, yes."

"You cutted yourself!
When you get oh, about fifty...
you'll feel it...
pain on your back
because you cutted it."

"What about you?"

"I'm your old-man but I'm telling you!
You dig yam?"

"Yes"

"Well one of your granny or mother
you digging through the belly.
You must cover im up, cover again.
When you get yam you cover
so no hole through there
because you killing yam other thing.
And you got to hang on..."

Nangarn, a tuber - *Bunkaniyal*, Maningrida 1979.

So I hang on.
If I go yam...I tell kid...
>"Who left that hole there?"

>"Oh we forget."

>"Go on...cover im up.
>If you leave im hole you killing yam
>or killing yourself...cover!
>You hang on for this your country; nobody else.
>That way I fight for.
>I got im...e's yours.
>I'll be dead...I'll come to earth."

That tree for us, for anybody
but some places they don't like it tree.
They say...
>"Oh that tree can cut down.
>Throw im out."

No.
Because that tree e cutting...that his feeling.
If we chop im that tree,
might be bad headache
or feel funny his body
because e cutting it our body.

Even grass.
Grass can burn when e dry; well e's no good.
We got to burn it because that King Brown,
e made fire that.

E said...
    "I'll burn im because e's finished.
    New one be coming..."

So im e bin burn but new grass coming.

Lorgun, carrying the bone coffin - Croker Is. 1967.

Fire is nothing when you burn it.
I want burn it fire
because always used to be burn before
and new grass coming up.
That mean good animal...might be goose,
goanna, bandicoot, possum.

They didn't want this rotten grass.
They say...
> *"Might as well rid of im.*
> *Burn im and new life,*
> *new grass coming up."*

No-matter grass im burn but roots there...e'll grow.
Even tree.
E burn leaf alright but e come back.

If young one, e'll come new one, e's still alive.
You can cut im down, top, but e'll come back again
because root e still alive.

If e burn whole lot...
doesn't matter...might be roots e got green.
New plant e come up...same tree!

Hollow tree e burn out and e's finished.
We get grey-hair, that tree e got hollow
because too old now so e'll burn.
Sometimes strong wind e go knock im over
because not enough strong now.

So you grow...old man now.
That tree e grow, getting old.
You can't see grey-hair but might be leaf e come off
because just about finish.
E might be got something...white-ants!

Well white-ants e like im...that bloke e eating it!
So strong wind...that tree e go. That tree say...
        "I'm just about old now.
          I'm finished."

Sometimes no leaf...
        "Ahh...this tree is finished.
          E dead wood this one."

So e can get im honey.
E can look bush-honey there...hollow tree.
You'll have to chop im down
Because you want that honey.
I mean bush-honey e can't get in that solid one
because you want hollow tree.

So we used to chop im down
because that tree just about finished.
E never cut more.

E can drive longa road, highway;
e can look big lumber there.
E don't go rotten because solid wood.
Bulldozer e killing it.
Well that feeling of me...something.

What for they cutting it land?
Because tree going down and that road e go.
Soon as bitumen there e don't grow any grass there.
That road e stay...no grass.
Side e's right but middle of it nothing.
You drive, you look lumber-stick there, big log there,
big 'dozer pull it out...
well your body you feel. You say...
        "Oh...that tree same as me!"

I look tree but I say...
        "Just like mother, father or brother,
        grandma."

'Course your granny, your mother, your brother
because this earth, this ground,
this piece of ground e grow you.

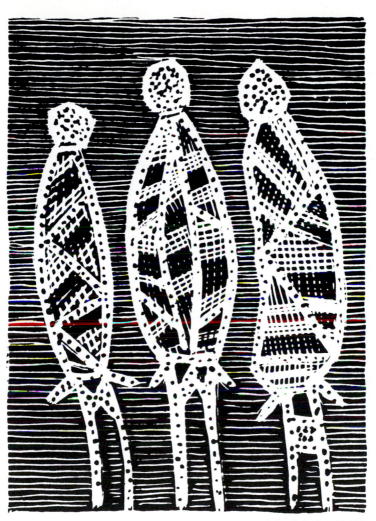

Unidentified - Oenpelli, 1948.

31

I drive. I see big lumber-log lying down.
That way you get pain on your back.
You know, that tree e push,
bulldozer e pull it out big roots.
That one e cut your back.
E should be stay in ground for us.
This tree...for us.

"Lovely tree", we say.
Well we say, "lovely man".
Young-fella, young man..."e lovely man".
Well we look lovely tree...all same.
"Oh beautiful bird"...colour, yes.
This ground or any river, flower...same thing.
Pretty colour snake...
"I seen it good colour snake".
Well same you'n'me.
"Good man that"...young-fella or young-girl...
all same.

Tree smooth.
What about you'n'me smooth skin?
Might be sunburn you but you got white, no-matter me.
But this the story. You can't split im,
you can't change im, you can't do anything.
This story you got to keep im...in your feeling.
Tree for us, eagle...anything.
Eagle, bird, animal, rock...this the story.

Creation story of three prominent rocks between Oenpelli and the sea
- *Mangudja*, Oenpelli 1967.

Because you pull it up from that earth this tree,
you feel it.
Not myself but everyone, anybody, no-matter who.
We all feel it.

This shade...we can sit down...hot!
I get it everyone. I get im good shade there.
You know why e can get im good shade there?
Because that tree is yours.
That tree e watching you, anyone, my story is.
Same as umbrella now, new.
But this tree was started I don't know how many year.
Might be million, million year this tree e grow.
E died off...e's alright, e'll come another one.

That tree e can grow because you need tree e grow.
E was growing before there.

That tree e grow there, smooth tree.
E starting might be dark, e get dark e start grow.
Well you can look...smooth tree!
Young tree e go through, e go about morning,
good smooth tree...

     "Hey...good tree!
      Oh nice tree this...smooth."

Because e started early.
Just about dark when e started.
That plant e grow smooth tree.
Another one e was growing late,
round about middle-night I think.
E grow...and daylight! So e's short, e got fork.
That tree e can tell you how e reached that daylight.

Stringybark e can look...
     "Ahh, lovely stringybark...smooth."

But halfway up e got fork. Why?
Because e daylight there.

Well that tree twelve hour e grow you can look...straight!
When e hit about daylight e spread out now.
You look little plants, you plant that watermelon...
e grow straight first, then leaf.
This same this tree e grow...daylight, e's finished.
E can't come back smooth tree
because that daylight e win you see!

Well some people they say...
"Lovely tree, look!"

But me...I think that story.

This tree e stay...watching you.
Something...this tree.
If you go by yourself, lie down,
that tree e can listen.
Might be e might give you signal.
Spirit...quiet e say...
"Oh, my man coming!"

Something...you know, noise.
You might say...
"Hey, what's that!"

We done like that before.
I was lying down. I listen stick!
Just like somebody breaking...I jump!
My grandpa...
"Don't that...tree."

"Oh. E broke here."

"E's no break...e spoke in sleep.
E won't hurt us. Might be somebody coming."

That signal.
Alright, we settle down, we stay there.
I was looking, laying down.
Next minute I seen it fire, somebody bin make fire.
"Hey fire there!"

My grandpa e said...
"Yes.
Well leave it...that's the tree now.
E tell you somebody coming.
That tree e work."

Alright...four of them,
from Oenpelli they bin walk, bring smokes,
little bit tea and sugar.
Anyhow, they bin come...
"Oh, must I tell story!
This tree e tell us you mob coming."

My uncle e said...
"Yes...e was like that before."

Well they told me story.

Turkey dance - *Narangorlgi,* Croker Is. 1967

WARRAMURRAUUNGI

And never forget in culture that story
Some caves written on this Woman
And you got to hang on when you dead
Because kid they can't lose im
Must hang on

40	That Woman brought up all this people
42	Eating
44	Hunting
45	Paperbark
46	She follow river..."Oh lily!"
47	Honey
48	Apples, plums and yams
49	So we can see goose in the plain
50	They used to live in caves there
	and come out, go hunting
51	Dingo e can tell
52	First lightning

Facing page: The Water Woman Likanaya sitting by the water singing magic songs against intrusion to the sacred waterhole Indjularrku near the Gumadeer River – Oenpelli 1976.

Spirit figures from cave paintings - Oenpelli 1971.

This story is one of the Woman, from Macassa I think.
Her name...Warramurrauungi.
So that story...e came from the sea.
Came up Mali Bay, north from here. *

That Woman brought up all this people.
E started Mali Bay each clan
Gunmurrgurrgurr they say, but my word,
my mother-word...Yiwurrum.
That: tribe-of-people.

*Malay Bay.

40

She started Manganawal tribe
and my wife is Manganawal.
Manganawal...e came Amurdak.
Next one...Ulbu, my mother-country.
Ulbu...and e came Gadurra,
other side this Arnhem Land, not far.
Gadurra...e came Gagudju now, my country, here.
Gagudju...e went Ulbu, Mbukarla, Bukurnidja,
but e left each people with lingo.

So e started...Woman.
And e was carrying kid.
E go amongst that place there,
e left group of them people.
Might be one-thousand something, might be more
and e just say...
    "You stay there."

That one group...and they build up more,
more people and even my people here, same.

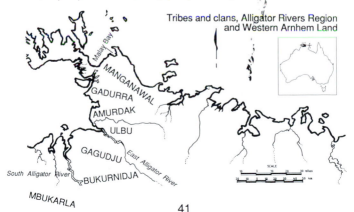

Tribes and clans, Alligator Rivers Region
and Western Arnhem Land

And e teach im. E said...
>"This: eating.
>Red-apple...anykind of tucker for the people.
>Anykind of tree, yam..."

E dig up one long yam, e seen it, e said...
>"This good tucker!"

E said...
>"Lily and lily-nuts,
>little one in the plains...they can dig up and eat."
>"What this track?
>What this track eh...I follow."

E follow that track...e find it.
>"Oh...long-neck turtle!
>What I do? I kill im!"

She killed that.
>"Oh, I better make a fire."

E made fire-stick. E cook it...
>"Oh lovely this."

E eat...
>"Oh fat! Oh people can eat."

So everybody looking for.
Hunting...

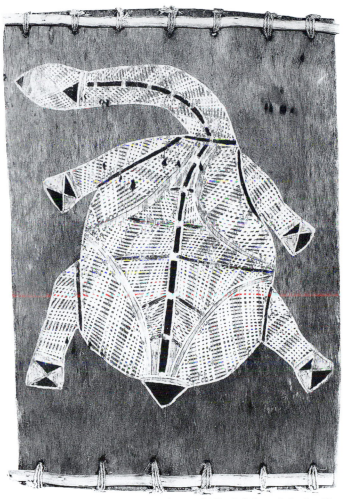

- unknown artist, Darwin Gallery collection item 58.

I go hunting.

You got to go hunting for long-neck turtle.
You got to go lily.
You got to go hunting for bush-honey.
You got to go.
She said...so we follow.

We can't change it because you got to carry on.
That our culture, our tucker...you can't lose.
You must go. You must hang on.
I see few Aborigine don't eat...
    "Oh we can't eat!"

I said...
    "Oh you silly.
     You not Aborigine. What you? White-European?
     This your tucker! What you talking about?"

I said...
    "You got to eat."

    "Oh we not used to it."

    "Oh silly!
     You'll be used to it to eat this.
     If you leave im...silly!
     Everyone for us.
     We came this world and you got to eat this stuff
     and e got flavour, everything."

She went get paperbark...just like blanket.
   "I wrap it up myself."

E wrap it up imself, cover up, go sleep.
That's the one we was cover up with paperbark.
You can't get wet, top,
unless water's running in the floor.
Dry place, high ground, you can't get wet.
You just cover up.
You'll be there till tomorrow if not move around.

She done it.

Bardayal Nadjamerrek, Oenpelli 1974.

"River...
  I follow river."

She follow river...
  "Oh, lily!"

She get handful lily. She eat it...
  "Oh I can eat this lily."

Raw she bin eat.
  "Alright, full now...throw im away.
    Let im grow."

So lily e can eat raw...some.
Because flavour for you.

Mankodbe, a tuber from a climbing vine with small
dark leaves. A staple food, many people could get
a meal from one fully developed plant
- *Bunkaniyal,* Maningrida 1979.

That's the one e left all this.
That Woman came...
She left each bird, goanna, lizard, any sort of a honey...

E walk, e turn, e see tree...
    "What this one here? What this?"

E take that rotten stick...e come down honey.
E taste it...
    "Ahh, this good honey.
    This one for Aborigine.
    Oh very sweet!"

E eat.
Alright e get paperbark...e cupside there.
E put water. E drink...
    "Oh sweet. Very good.
    People can drink and eat that honey."

So honey e can eat straight away off the tree
or e can take im home.
E can put in that water...same as like tea eh!
Same thing because flavour for you
and clean your stomach.
I used to drink that water because e can clean you,
clean you up...
good medicine!

E went see apple...
>"Ahh, here apple. Good one I think."

E taste it...
>"Ahh good one! People can eat."

Plum.
Any sort of a some yam...little one buried.
This one 'cheeky yam'. E said...
>"No good! That brown one plenty here.
> This one e can soak im all night,
> till next morning."

E won't kill you but sour.
But e can throw im in the water
e can eat im next morning...oh lovely.

Right. She gone for yam.
She bin dig up eat half...
>"Oh I'll cook some."

So long yam e can dig up, e can eat raw
and e can take im cook im if you want to.
Because that mean, raw, e can eat...
that flavour for you.
Make more blood and clean your body.
When you eat cook...same thing, clean your stomach.

We can't leave im because She said...so we follow.
We can't leave im, we can't change,
unless we little bit too much busy now.
So sometimes we don't eat honey, sometimes we eat.

If you pick im up now, lily, you can eat.
Yam you can dig up.
You got to eat because...
      "Never forget!"

I'm teaching all these kids.

And e make this, that Woman.
E made this world.

E walking along there.
E said...
      "Oh, lizard, blue-tongue lizard!
      This one good eating and what this one here?
      Oh this one goose. Ahh...people can eat goose."

Because She make everything that.
She pointed...
      "Look...goose!"

So we can see goose in the plain.

Yams and tubers, all good food: left - Karrbirlk, bottom - Burda, centre - Bajdju, top - Manngalinj - *Bunkaniyal,* Maningrida 1979.

"Stone...this rock...its yours.
In the dry e can go hunting.
In the wet-season e got to come back in cave.
Save you building houses."

They used to live in caves there
and come out, go hunting.
They used to live all over, follow each billabong.
Lilies, lily-roots and ordinary lily again, big mobs
and long-neck turtle and this goose...
"Goose...never leave.
E can eat, people can eat."

She bin clean that goose and eat.

So before...we used to get with stick.
They fly for water or feeding ground...

"Look how they fly.
Alright...I'll make camp there under."

Time...you wait there.
When they fly, knock em down one by one.
Might be fifteen or ten goose enough,
big family, might be twenty.
Never miss. Each stick. I seen it myself.
We used to pick im up that stick
and take im back in the water
because still weight there...heavy, you know.
They used to say...
        "If you leave im out there, day,
        you can't hit goose.
        That stick be light!
        So chuck im in the water.
        Save you wasting that stick."

I said...
        "We can cut im new one."
        "No! You can't cut new one.
        You cutting all that tree
        and cutting yourself."

So we used to follow. We used to hang on that stick
might be two, three months.
Each morning we used to throw im back before sunrise.
Might be fifteen stick...fifteen geese...never miss.
This time...easy. You know, shotgun.
But other thing...you frighten im.
They go too wild!

Dingo e can tell.
E yelling out in the night because you can listen.
That story...e was walking down.
Next minute e listen...
      "Ahh dingo...poor thing."

So people can listen dingo, everybody.
E can listen in the night
or you can see im walking along
but e too wild you know.
      "I can't touch you because you wild."

So e look wild. She done it.
If we get im we breed im...alright, e go quiet.
Because She never get that dingo...so that rule now.
That's the story She made.
If I get young one...alright.
But big one you can't get im because She said,
      "No! Nobody can touch...
        but e can listen."

That dingo over there she want to cry in the night
because other one over there...give signal.
E say, "Come on...might be dead buffalo over there".
So this one e might be hungry,
so they come, big mob and they eat.
E can smell im too. E can smell us. E say, "Man".

Because that story.
She made all this story.

I call im Gunwandul
South...first lightning.
You can't see first lightning all over north or east
because no more allow.
That Woman she seen it first.

From my father that story...Gunwandul.
He belong to that story there.
E told me...
"What lightning e can see over there?"

Thunder spirit with hammers and lightning -
artist deceased, Oenpelli 1971.

"No. I can't see lightning there.
 Why? Why can't get lightning over there?"

"Because that Woman seen it first-lightning
 so you can't see over north or east
 not allowed!
 If e change...
 first rain this way, lightning...
 something wrong!
 Got to be first-rain, lightning there.
 Always...no-matter what!"

That Woman e gone here.
E was sitting down because e seen it first-lightning...
        "Hey what's that?
         Oh...lightning!"

She bend down.
She was going to go south...
        "I stay here because lightning there.
         What for lightning?"

So e bend down, move her head...
        "Oh, I see.
         I look lightning.
         I put it down because shame."

She bend down.

E can look each people, no matter who is.
Woman or kid, young-fella, anyone,
e always put it down his head
because that Woman she made that story.
So each kid e put it down his head.
E can't look that man because shame.

Lightning spirit Yowg-Yowg - *Gubargu,* Maningrida 1971.

The Kangaroo-woman rainmaker - unknown artist, Oenpelli 1948

RAIN

E want that new water
So fish, turtle e can make new one
Because that story

58   This cloud for us
59   Big Barra from salt water
60   E come along wet...e go dry
61   That way first rain

X-ray fish - *Midjau Midjau*, Croker Island 1967.

Sky...
this cloud for us.
Your story, my story.

Yes anybody can see cloud
because e bring new water,
making more new water for us.

Rain for us, anybody.
Rain e give us because something.
Water for us.

Rain e'll come down because Warramurrauungi said that.
We can't be going dry, dry...
because that lightning e give us water.
That Woman done it.

Female Munimunigan spirit with sweptback hairstyle
- unknown artist, Oenpelli 1948.

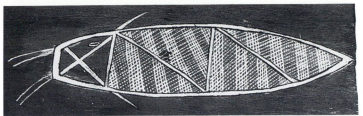

What e do rain?

E raining because e give us something
new...what you eating it.
Yam, fish, anykind animal e give you...wet-season.
E drop im something there because story.
You can find good barra in the wet or after the wet
because that water.

Water running down in the stream...
Big-barra e follow that fresh-water.
Big-barra e travel, e come, keep going, get in fresh...
　　　"Oh fresh here! Keep going, can't stop."

Because shallow part e lay and drop.
E want that fresh.
Big-barra from salt-water.

Because...rain helping.
Something made there.
E can make eggs, mussels, anykind
but must have rain!
If you can't get rain what happen to us?
Something be happen!
You must get im because Law says you get rain.

E changing it now.
All this tree e changing it new leaf
because e got to come new rain.
Same any sort of a plant...e coming up new.
Yam e'll come too.
Yam, creeper, any bush-creeper e's growing
because that meaning of that Woman and that Man.
They made story
and this King-Brown.
They said...
     "This e got to grow each year before wet."

One rain...you look grass e come.
E got something this top water here,
e throw something there.
First rain one, each billabong e drop down dry.
E want that new water so fish, turtle,
e can make new one.

E come along wet...e go dry.
Because that dry, e make im dry, e said...
     "People be staying inside
     and dry be going out for hunting.
     They can eat, look animal.
     E looking for himself.
     Snake...e can find himself because story.
     Little lizard, little bird...
     e looking for something to eat."

Snake or anykind...wet.
Blue-tongue lizard...no-matter what is animal, we animal,
we human being but this the story now.
Any sort of a animal...same we.
Animal not himself...we too.

We might look around
because that dream e started looking for.
E said...
> "Well you must go get your fruit or honey
> or something to eat, keep you alive.
> Water e'll come down give you new fresh water."

That way first rain.

Visit to the spirit world - *Mangudja,* Oenpelli 1967.

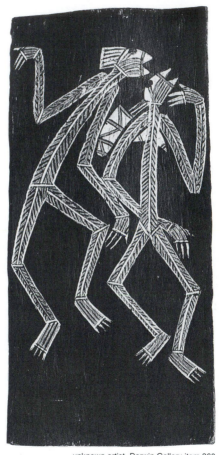

-unknown artist, Darwin Gallery item 360.

NO HISTORY FOR US

"Well, we'll be dead
And they can see our painting
Because behind us all the children...right back
They can keep on look this painting and bone
They can see us if they behind us."

65	Good mob was there that day now
67	They used to paint themselves alright!
68	So only in cave
71	"Well no culture. You forget!"

Spirit people attacking a man - Oenpelli 1971.

Because what I think you know,
I was thinking...no history for us before,
when they start any European here...
Paddy Cahill, Joe Cooper, Rodney Spencer,
Baldwin Spencer...and only few word written on.
Should be more than that...way Aborigine was live.
Few you know.

Good mob was there that day now.
I bin grow up but them lot...oh, wicked!
Never do little bit wrong...
get spear straight away.
They cheeky mob.
But all bin dead.
Now...easy! This mob here they easy.
Few people but easy.
That mob dead...
oh me...I fright!

And trouble is they didn't like each other.
I don't know why.

They should have bin stay
like might be same place same.
They didn't like other people.
Other people they didn't like this mob,
this mob they didn't like that mob...
I don't know why.

They used to go one hunting place.
They used to come down, say...
   "You can't go hunting there, that mine!"

Start fight.
I don't know why.
They keep it from each...secret.
They didn't want ten-mile company
or five-mile to come down easy.
Unless one manager e say...
   "Come on. We eat."

Flood-plain.
That plain of hunting-place.

My mother, my grandad, my father was hunting there
and wasn't in no clothes.
Spear they use...ironwood,
carry around little bit of net, short net.

The man Waraguk - unknown artist, Oenpelli 1948.

They used to paint themselves alright...Aborigine.
No white-man...nobody was Balanda.
They used to paint themselves
because wasn't ordinary paint.

They was lying down with that fire longside.
I saw couple of men doing it like that.
I painted myself. They said...
> *"Put it on this one. Rub yourself.*
> *Go sleep over there."*

I was about 14 years old.
I sleep there. Next morning I said...
> "What for I done I sleep there?
> What for I put paint?"

> *"All that string...*
> *that's like rubbing medicine.*
> *You doing it rubbing medicine.*
> *That paint e take what you got sick inside,*
> *cold or gas, that paint will take im.*
> *All lot, all the sore, headache..."*

I was little bit sick too and true he told me my grandpa.
 E said...
> *"That's the one paint.*
> *That medicine for you."*

I didn't know.

So this time I know but we don't go, we don't tell im
because they only follow White-European medicine.
But medicine good for the kid.

They got little bag.
They put it in a cave...long time.
Can't find im now.
They try looking for...couldn't find im that medicine
because you can't see where camping area Aborigine.

They never making camp how we camping here.
Aborigine before...they use paperbark, stringybark
and soon as fire...e burn everything,
clothes and paperbark.

So only in cave...well that painting.
We don't know how many thousand years
that painting was there.
Our Aborigine never writing, no date, no anything.
No one bin make everything...
only painting and stone-axe.
Ironwood-spear, bamboo...all burn, you can't see.
Painting you know is there because dry
and never get wet.

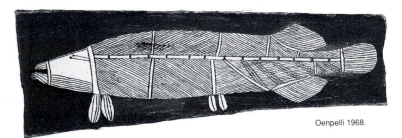

Oenpelli 1968.

Saucer rock, saucer plate...plenty there...*
Well you know, they was mincing it.
Mince plum or any hard meat.
Any sort of a thing, hard one, they mince.
Make im soft for old people you see.
Plum, goanna tail, wallaby tail they used to mince.
Just like soup...well good soup!
Only that soup e new day one.

Before...no boiling.
They used to roast im that's all
and cook im in the coals.
They used to cook im alright...put im in the hot stone,
e cook straight away.
They never make a fire longa rock
because that stone crack, you know.
E get hot...e bust! You get burnt.
Mostly, you know, bit of dirt...they used to make a fire.

And that way they left that story. They said...
"Well, we'll be dead
and they can see our painting
because behind us all the children...right back.
They can keep on look this painting and bone.
They can see us if they behind us.
This country for us."

* Grinding hollows occur in rock shelters at Kakadu.

Spirit man and kangaroo - Oenpelli 1971.

So some painting you can see wallaby,
catfish, mullet, file-snake, water-python,
might be goanna, might be crocodile,
might be fresh-water crocodile.
Because...that's the one all good tucker that.

Except King-brown...no one draw
because that's the one they said...
> *"Oh very bad!"*

Because e kill anybody.
Kill Aborigine, kill white-man, kill yellow, kill black.
E can kill im because e's poison...e's no good.

But all 'eating one' they got here...Ubirr.
Possum, rock-wallaby little one, big one
and black-kangaroo.

Bit hand and spear, and big fight they bin draw.
String...woman with string.

Because that string, that for corroboree,
always for corroboree.
When they used to finish that corroboree,
put it away string in her bag...
put it away and wrap im up with paperbark.

Now they got handbag and suitcase now
and you can't hardly see...no string in that!
Got in suitcase now...powder, comb
but should be string or anykind for Aborigine.
I never see one
but should be.
I said...
        "Well no culture. You forget!"

Woven dilly bags, one with painted feather decoration; woven, painted
and feathered string girdle - unknown artists, Maningrida 1971.

White paint they drawing...clay.
White clay and yellow clay.
That yellow...
They used to get im special one I think
because e got little bit of oil in it.
But we looking for, we never see, we can't find im.
Just like paint and lovely yellow.
I don't know where they used to get it.

That red clay too.
Wasn't rock this one...all smooth like flour.
Just put a handful and that's it.

I couldn't find im. I don't know.
My grandpa...
I never ask im that.

Facing page:
Namarrkon the maker of storms, Lightning Man. His camp is the top of a great
red cliff with a pool below, and none may cut any trees there for fear of his anger
and a flood - or that the person be killed by lightning. Here he is angered and lifting
up the rainbow is about to throw it across the sky, singing and dancing to summon
the great winds, cumulus clouds, rain and lightning. In this area, a clever man
who knows a certain rock may strike it and call the power names of this big man,
making rain fall. Such a clever man would also carry magic rain stones
in special bags - Oenpelli 1973.

73

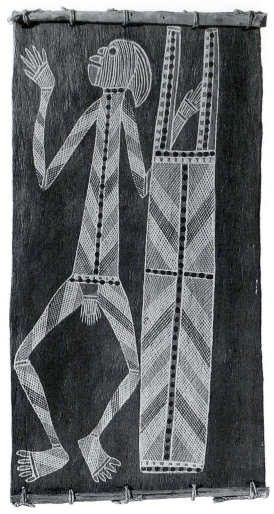

Lorgun, man with bone coffin - Oenpelli 1971.

Some dead people because big mob people.
They used to take im back in the cave.
This time, people dying now...in coffin.
But coffin they not supposed to, Aborigine.
Take im back where e belong and put in that something!

They used to put up bones.
Soon as ready...pick im up and take im to the cave.
Because they was saying...
>"Well e got to stay with his spirit."

If people, if you go in the cave, you must yell out.
Give signal because if you've got new man with you,
new man might be stranger...you got to yell out.

Each place, no-matter here, all over...
they doing like that because otherwise you get sick.
You know, Aborigine, that's all.
You might get sick or very bad sick
because wrong spot, wrong place.
Signal, must signal, sing out first
because they used to tell us...
>"Yes...your father, your grandad, your aunty,
>they'll be waiting for you.
>You must signal, yell out...they'll listen.
>They know you. They will know.
>So that stranger man they can't hurt im."

Because that's the dream...

Orion and the Pleiades, the three fishermen Burum-burum-runja. The circular design is the fire, with flames and smoke - unknown artist, Groote Eylandt 1948.

76

DREAMING

Should be forty-five pounds or eighty
Eighty pounds easy!
Barra like that
Easy!

79   Where the feeling coming from
80   Just about like Djang
85   I think we spoiling our fish

Three fish - Croker Is. 1967.

This story not for myself...all over Australia story.
No-matter Aborigine, White-European, secret before,
didn't like im before White-European...

This time White-European must come to Aborigine,
listen Aborigine and understand it.
Understand that culture, secret, what dreaming.

Big name...'dreaming'.
Dreaming e listen. E say...
    "Exactly right!"

Because that dreaming made for us.

This Indjuwanydjuwa...
Two way e made. E said...
        "I want rain. I want people.
         Oh! Something I forget!
         I'll have to make im something.
         They can grow but must keep im this..."

So e made that 'Business'. 'Business' for people.

Well they got Bible they say
but this man, Indjuwanydjuwa, e said...
        "I put this one here and star.
         You got something to think about
         and show young fellas."

They want to know where the feeling coming from.
That thing now. You know...
Another secret, another secret, another one secret,
another one, another one...
all that feeling e come to you, feeling...now.
Me or you or somebody else...samething.
All same.

E said...
      "I make this one...but secret!
      No kid, no woman, no young fella,
      unless they get in that Ring-place before e can
      see."

I can't call im...because no good.
I just saying this 'outside'.
'Inside' things I can't call im because not in Law.
Got to be in Ring-place before e can see!

Because half of it...I went away myself.
My father e pass away and I follow my mother,
right down the sea.
I stay. I went away between 1928-29.
1979 I back in Cannon-Hill.
So I just work it out what secret place, important place,
Ring-place and show these children.
I done half of it there because children will look after.

Because the Law...
      "No-one walk through, walk close there!"

I can't make any camping area there
because no good for anybody...
no-matter my Aborigine, no-matter White-European
because Law...
      "Got to be stay out!"

That old people they told us.
They told me to stay out any Ring-place because...

I said...
      "What for?"
      "No-matter we dead
      but that Law you got to keep it.
      No one can go in there
      make fire or camping."

Can't break Law.
The Ring-place must stay way e started
because that Ring-place is important,
just about like Djang...dreaming place.
And you can't change it no-matter anyone,
no-matter rich man whatever,
no-matter is King, whatever King
but that Law e can't break.
Ring-place e can't go through.

Secret. That Djang.
We say, "Djang". Our lingo..."Djang".
That secret place...dreaming there.

We fright. Might be something there.
You might get hurt or you might spoil something there.

You might spoil anybody, no-matter where.
Same as cyclone, if you spoil it. First one might be east,
no-matter Croker, Elcho or Brisbane...same.
That Djang now will do it because Djang e not small,
Djang is biggest one.

We sitting on top that Djang.
You sitting on this earth but something under,
under this ground here.
We don't know. You don't know yourself.
I don't know myself but that story.

Because that Djang we sitting on under,
e watching, that Djang, what you want to do.
If you touch it you might get heavy cyclone,
heavy rain, flood or e kill in another place...
other country e might kill im.

That why we fright little bit we can stop im mining.
Oh, some mining might be alright...this Ranger mine
but we said...

       "You try. E might be alright."

E try it...it's alright, only people they worry about,
that's all. Because that King Brown.
But anyhow, too late for us, too late...e can see it.
But that Djang...King Brown dream.

Balanda!
If Aborigine e says something, if e get little bit wild,
you know...e want to stop im Balanda...e might listen.
But slow e got to ask im...
"What that Djang there?"

Because some Aborigine they hang on.
They don't want to tell im.
They won't tell im story easy.

But this story is true this one.
Secret might be e kill somebody or something come out
or kill other place or wind.
That way they fright.

Some sores...what we call 'mia mia'
but this one, 'mia mia', biggest...just like boil.
So one dreaming over there, rock
but if you touch e kill straight away...very bad.
So we're watching so nobody can go.

Because first people, old people, they said...
"Don't go touch it.
If you go touch it you won't get better
because you only killing yourself!"

So that way secret.

We say, "Djang".
English...what you say?

You know Djang...because might be important.
Might be no good for you,
no good for me because that story.
They said...
> "No good for anybody!"

If you can't listen, European, to Aborigine...
you go there, something wrong...well your own fault
because you breaking Law you see.
No-matter White-European...this story same!

Someone in your country there,
something happen there...
what you feel like?
You might be feel yourself...worry. You won't say.
Any Aborigine feeling,
they doing like that because I know.
E just feeling himself. E worry slow and e get very weak.
E won't say...
> "Hey! What for you done..."

E won't!

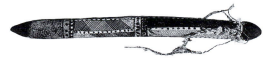

Yam stick - Croker Is. 1967.

They might say e can change im.
No. You can't change im. Never change.
Because e started that Djang and we keep on.

We can't say...
    "Djang over there."

And they liar...
    "No. E not Djang there."

Barramundi in the fire. "In the dreamtime Nagorku took the barramundi dreaming along the coast from Cape Don and into the rivers and creeks" - *Milaybuma,* Maningrida, 1971.

We say Djang there
because She bin make im that Djang.
So we follow.
I can't say that Djang over there no good, not worth it
because that Djang She made. So I hang on.
They said...

> *"Well this you hang on.*
> *Djang is Djang.*
> *E made that Djang*
> *and you got to be well look after."*

But this Djang is there alright because dream made that.
So we don't know, might be important.
Might be you only spoil it world or spoiling our eating.

I think we spoiling our fish; other thing.
And some animal we spoiling it
because some animal don't like something
so they go away.
Some animal they like im what we doing,
some animal don't like im...bird or anything.
Some fish they do that because we got taught.
They tell us...

> *"Fish...*
> *we got to cook it carefully.*
> *Don't touch fish too rough!"*

"What for?"

"Because dream...that Barra.
If you too rough, other fish is feeling
because that fish you got to eat
and half of fish your body.
E got flavour to make good.
You spoiling it when you cook it rough way,
you got to eat cooked properly way.
Half raw and you throw it away...
that mean next day you can't get fish!"

"Because what for?"

"Because She said.
That Woman said don't waste it.
You got to eat fish.
You must not throw back in the river...
other fish e won't come."

So I said over here, Border Store...
    "You get fish...don't throw im back!"

So few tourists might be they bin throw.
You only get little fish. They say...
    "Why little fish?"

    "I don't know. I can't explain to you
    because you won't understand what I'm saying.
    If you want to get little one, that's for you
    but I know what happened."

They throw head, bone...
because Barramundi dreaming over here.

You might get new rain, good water...
you might get good size
but that bone, head...burn im!
Because our people they used to eat whole lot,
head and all and burn im...
never throw im back in the river.
Other fish they say, "Oh!"

Because that thing. That Woman she said...
     "Don't throw our bone in the creek
      because you can't get fish good size."

But big mobs they throw in river.
Now you get little one, about seven pounds that's all.
Should be forty-five pounds or eighty,
eighty pounds easy!
Barra like that, easy!
About twenty-five, forty-five they get im here few.
I said...
     "No. That only small barra that.
     Not enough weight. Should be more than that."

Oenpelli 1968.

You might dream moon,
or you might dream water, storm.

You might dream tree, wind.   Kakadu - *Ian Morris.*

KING BROWN
AND THAT LAW OF OOBARR

This outside story
Anyone can listen, kid, no matter who
But that inside story you can't say
If you go in Ring-place, middle of a Ring-place
You not supposed to tell im anybody
But oh e's nice!

Oobarr they made...
King Brown and that water-snake, water python.

Spirit people and python in cave - Oenpelli 1967.

E was his wife and e didn't like im much. *
Some woman e don't like man e like other man.
That's the trouble...this woman here for King Brown.

King Brown I say English but 'Irwardbad' Aborigine name.
Irwardbad e made that story...

E went in big hollow tree. E was lying down.
E made fire and e clean up right round.
Ashes where e burn.

So this Mother and her daughter...
    "Hey! Come on!"

That young woman she bin come...
    "Eee! Look...flat!
    Might be goanna or something.
    Might be possum or...
    We kill im! Might be bandicoot!"

E look...
    "Ahh there! I can see his eye."

Hollow tree.
That mother one used to look through
and this King Brown used to shut his eye.
Soon as young girl used to look...
    "Ahh there! E watching me!"

Because his wife. Should be.

* E...e: here the feminine.

That King Brown e said...
> "I got to grab im."

That young girl used to put arm, feel it there.
E bin bite her hand!
> "Mum! E bite me."

That old woman used to feel there. No, e never bite im.
Only that young girl, she feel it...bang, finger!
> "Yes e bite me!
> Come on mummy, your turn!"

> "Ahh I better kill im this old lady too.
> No-matter my cousin but I'll have to kill im."

> "Ayee! E bite me alright."

Finish!
> "I got sore finger now."

And they bin start look funny now, drunk.
That snake e bin come out, look.
E said...
> "No-matter.
> You never like me. You didn't like me.
> I kill anybody, no-matter who is. I kill im."

That two bin get sick...

"You finished?"

"No."

"Mummy! What we do?"

"We can't do anything."

"Well we got to go back where daddy!"

"No. We can't make it.
We bin find im something here...poison!
I'm getting weak now. I don't think so we can walk."

That King Brown e bin look that two...

"I go back fix im up?"

E bin walk close. Stand up. Look...

"More better I fix im up that two, poor thing.
No! That woman e never come close to me.
That woman she hard, hard for me.
She never come near."

That snake e going. E turn round, look...

"Oh, more better I go fix im up."

Three times e come back. Stand up. Change mind...

"Hey you two!
No! I'll leave it. I'd better go."

They bin vomiting.

That snake e bin go up Cooper's Creek.
E bin sit down, lay down, roll over, swing, stand up head,
crawl round...that snake e bin play!
E bin go, go that snake...
make im clear place now, like airstrip!
Alright. That snake bin stop now.
King Brown e said...
   "Might be that two woman finished, they dead."

E didn't know.
E bin get im didgeridoo.
E bin get im, stand im up...
   "People...no-matter what country.
   E got to use im this didgeridoo.
   And what this clear place?
   Oh! This one for Oobarr!"

So we got it. E made that. That for Oobarr.
So we say Ring-place, nobody can look, nobody can go.
Because e himself, King Brown said...
   "Nobody can look."

Only old people where they go Oobarr...they know.
They allowed to go.
Young kid, woman...no-more allowed.
They got another place.
They got woman Ring-place over there.

Alright.
E going now...
 "Where I got to go?
 I go south. No! Something went there before me.
 No good I'm going. What about this road, north?
 No! Something there too.
 More better I go this way...east!"

E gone.
E listen...
 "Hey! Big mob people here!"

E going close. E look...
 "People alright! What I do?
 No good I'm walking, they might look me.
 I turn around myself eh!"

E bin lay down.
E bin crawl alright.
E went like snake. E said...
 "Oh you mob can sit down
 but I crawl. You can't look me."

That mob, big mob, they was sitting down.
Snake was travelling. E gone middle.
Only one man e said...
 "Hello! Heart-crack!"

Like sometime you sleep or sit down...feel heart-crack.
You feel something..."I got man missing!"

This earth for us.
Just like mother, father, sister.

Cannon Hill, Kakadu - *Greg Miles.*

"Something went through here.
Hey! Snake! Snake!"

Too late.
"I go get im stick. I kill im snake here!"

E bin come back...nothing, only track...
"Where these two women?"

His wife and daughter!

His mother...
"They was here. They getting it lily!"

So e walk...see track.
"Hey, here fresh track. They went this way."

E follow that track.
E seen it crow and hawk they was circle round...
"Hey! What that hawk doing there?
E might be watch that two...I'd better go!"

That man e walk straight.
E look down that two woman there...e run!
"Hey! What's wrong?
Something bin kill im!"

E look mark and e seen it that hollow tree.
E bin think about...

"Ahh, might be this man!
   E bin do it himself I think."

E bin look track...
   "Ahh, King Brown alright!"

That man e follow that track. Follow, follow...
   "Hey! Clear place! What this?"

E look didgeridoo. E was thinking...
   "Oh...might be Oobarr!
   Something! Leave im!"

E went back got that two woman. E went home...
E put it down spear. Sitting down quiet...
   "Hey that one quiet. Where other two?
    Hey! What happened your wife and daughter?"
   "They finished!"
   "And this Man...where e gone?"
   "I don't know. E turn I think!"   *

They bin frightened...
   "Hey! That bloke might be King Brown.
    E might kill us! E kill us alright!"

They bin make im Oobarr.   **
Everyone bin go there, make that Oobarr
and they bin look that didgeridoo...
   "Hey! Oobarr alright!"

98

And everyone they bin know.

> "Hey you woman go one side.
> Young man, you can't go.
> Soon as old people they say "yes", you can go.
> You can't go there break Law. They might kill you.
> This...Oobarr. If you wrong they kill you.
> You must do it proper because King Brown.
> E made that Law and you can't change im."

You never change Oobarr.
Way e made, start up...still going right.
Nobody can change, no-matter who!
Head-man or might be manager, top-man,
might be boss-man
e can't change it we say
because that Law...King Brown made that.
E got to go for might be ever and ever...I don't know.

I went in front.
They tell me...

> *"This thing you can't tell im kid,*
> *you can't tell im friend,*
> *you can't tell im anybody, even your wife.*
> *You find your son...*
> *you can't tell im story about Oobarr,*
> *you got to tell im what I'm telling you now."*

Facing page:
* Turned into Irwardbad, the King Brown snake.
** They made the ceremony Oobar for King Brown spirit.

Might be you only spoil it world.

Saltwater crocodile, Kakadu - *Ian Morris.*

This 'outside' story.
Anyone can listen, kid, no-matter who
but that 'inside' story you can't say.
If you go in Ring-place, middle of a Ring-place,
you not supposed to tell im anybody...
but oh, e's nice!

This story you follow.
All bin dead long time ago, old man.
One thousand, might be forty-two thousand year...
same story this.
E made this story so we following.
I following now.

Oobarr too hard to change.
You know, like 'outside'
you can change tucker or anything,
clothes e can change im
but in Ring-place...never change.
You change im inside there, you get killed there.
Because King Brown I think made all this dreaming,
well we fright!
We say, "might be", you know.
But some White-European they don't listen,
they only worry about money.

I only explain White-European...

No good man e can't listen because e's no good,
e's feeling something else...even Aborigine.
Man like you, like me, you feeling with this story.
What I'm saying, you listen.
You'll feel your string, you feel your body,
you'll feel yourself.
Might be morning, you feeling...
"Ahh, I want to understand that. I want to listen."

In yourself...feeling.

But this story should be never lose.
E should be stay for might be million, million year...
with the country, with the people.
Because that story that Man made...
"Never change!"

Law e said...
"Never change!"

So we can't.
Something holding you, you see. You can't do it.
Word e can do it but that something...you can't do it.

We men...women too.
They got im because She made that.
They can't tell us, we can't tell im.
E Ring-place, our Ring-place
because that's the Law e made...King Brown.

If you go Ring-place...look different there,
different from here.
When you finished from bush you'll be start crying.
You don't want to come back in 'outside'
because everything got to be left there.
That Man e done it everything there, e left it in the bush.
When they make this Kunapipi, *
that King e'll come out himself.
When we finished...e disappeared.
I don't know where e go. You'll be start looking for.
If another Kunapipi, e'll come...same thing.

This time Balanda they say...
      "No you can't. I don't think you can make it!"

Because they don't prove it.
But Aborigine...
      "E's there alright...easy!"

But they won't say because Law.
In 'inside' left it there and we leave it.
This 'outside' I'm saying now...that nothing.
Woman or kid or anyone e can talk again.
Anyone can listen this I speaking.

But never change I say.
This culture belong to us.
In our body with this, this story.

---

* "Kunapipi: The sacred ground is the Mother Place through which men pass
  to be reborn." Berndt, The World of the First Australians.

This the one now...that star.
You look that star. E working that star,
working...
E go pink, e go white...
that King Brown eye!

E said...
"My eye can stay there...people can look."

King Brown e made that eye.
E went longa bush...e made that Ring-place.

Oobarr ritual - Croker Is. 1967.

And you know how Frill-neck Lizard can look funny?
Right...
Frill-neck Lizard e was good smooth animal.
Man. E man.

What e done...e look ugly now,
skinny tail, skinny leg, arm
and big one ear, frill neck...
e broke that Law of Oobarr!
So they tell im...
>"You broke Law.
> People be seeing you
> you'll look skinny; you won't grow more."

They open up his ear...
>"You'll be like that for ever and ever."

>"You can make me back way I was?"

>"No! Because Oobarr.
> You break Law, so we can't.
> You got to stay like that .
> You break Law for us."

So Oobarr...we can't break Law.
Never change. No because Law.
That Frill-neck Lizard e done it first
and you can look how im thin.
Too thin his arm, leg because his own fault.
E went in longa Oobarr and e spoil it.
They tell im...
>"We can't. You done it now.
> You spoil it. So we can't."

Spirit woman - Oenpelli 1971.

SPIRIT

You listen my story and you will feel im
Because spirit e'll be with you
You cannot see but e'll be with you e'll be with me
This story just listen careful

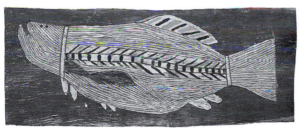

Mullet - Oenpelli   1964.

Jabiru nest...e's a dream.

That...
E made only nest there and e left it.
E said...
> "I near river. Creek here
> but I want nest make here."

And e made it then.

Is strongly story that Jabiru.
But something in spirit with the Jabiru.
That Jabiru got story.
If you think about, think about...you'll dream.
You'll dream of that nest or Jabiru
because you can feeling.
You, yourself, feeling.
And that Jabiru nest will come in to you.
And e say...
> "Ahh...e like me!"

E know.
E listen to you.
You can hardly look but e listen to you.
Alright, e come to you...you dream.
Your dream is real because your spirit is true.
And something e might drop im to you.
E might give you something.
Might be piece of rock you might find im
because spirit is there.

I love it too.
Is true...e can give you easy
because e longside you with this story.
I'm telling you but e longside with you.
How you feel...wind, feeling cold, "oh lovely night."
Yes...because e longside with you.
E listen to you this.

Jabiru...Badbanarrwarr.
That spirit of that Badbanarrwarr, Jabiru,
e'll be longside to you.
If you listen to this story here,
e'll be with you e'll be with me.
This story for me, for anybody, for you too.

I'll keep it this story about this dream
and you'll get it because spirit e'll be longside.
I'm telling it now but I'm longside.
I can feel it wind, blowing wind.

This one we say, "Only nest"
but not really.
That rock, nest, sitting on near plain over there, river
but something went in,
went under ground where the spirit for us.

That spirit e watching us.
For you and me that spirit.
Never lose. Always with us.
With you'n'me.

Dreaming places...Jabiru, Turkey, Barramundi,
little island, some billabong...but this the one.
This man e said...

    "Must keep it.
    You must keep im story
    because e'll come through your feeling.
    Even anybody."

E can see...have a look!

E not story.
I give you story alright
but that thing with our spirit and I only explain.
That rock e got to stay for might be million, million year.
E stay, e can't move.
That story with it and spirit with it.
We got spirit our story and spirit with us.

Turkey dance - Croker Is. 1967.

E special spirit for us.
You might dream.
I don't know but you might find something.
I find it couple of time in my pocket.
You might do that because is longside with you.
Or e can feel it your hair...
because e might be standing behind your back
or longside, sitting.
While you listen this story,
e might be longside with you and you feeling.
You say...
     "Oh! I bit fright. My hair is standing!"

No. Don't be fright, because hair e got to stand.
E don't have to hard-jump or something
because e with you.
E tell you...
     "Listen! Listen! Listen that story!"

E like it. E like.

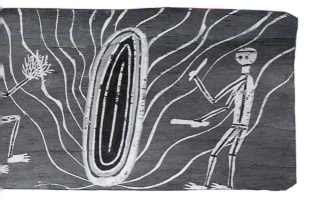

You cannot see.
I cannot see but you feel it.
I feel it.
E can feeling.
I feeling.

Spirit longside with you.
You sit...e sit. Telling you.
You think...
"I want to go over there."

E tell im you...before!
Anything you want to look...
"Ahh...go tree."

The Mopoke Men wearing feathers.
Men transformed into night birds
- unknown artist, Oenpelli 1948.

But e say...
"Hey! You go look that tree.
Something e got there."

You look...well you look straight away.
You might look snake, you might look bush-honey.
E telling you to have a look...
"Look up!"
"Ahh...bush-honey there."

Alright, you say...
"I go somewhere else. I go look painting."

All that painting, small mark...
they put cross, cross and over again.
White, yellow and little bit charcoal, little bit red clay...
that's the one all small meaning there.
They put it meaning.
They painting fish.. little mark they make im, you know.
That's the one same as this you look newspaper.
Big mob you read it all that story,
e telling you all that meaning.
All that painting now, small,
e tell im you that story.

That meaning that you look...you feel im now.
You might say...
      "Hey! That painting good one!
      I take im more picture."

That spirit e telling you...
      "Go on...you look."

Taking picture.

Well all that meaning there.
E say mother, granny, grandpa, grass, fire, bird, tree.
All that small thing, little thing,
all that mark they make it, when you go sleep
you dream...
going through your feeling.
You might sleep. Well you feel...
      "Hey, I bin dream good dream!"

White paint might be big hawk...before.
Yellow clay where sunset...e tell im you that secret.
You got to put im on yellow clay
because all that dream, all that story is there.
You got to put charcoal
because e got "business" there, what we call Dhuwa.
Yellow clay...Yirridtja.
Well all that piece, piece they paint im, all that story
secret, grandpa, granny, back, chest, head...
e coming through your feeling.
That painting you say...
    "That lovely painting."

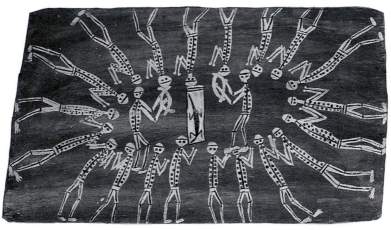

Lorgun, dancing around the coffin - Croker Is. 1967.

114

Finger prints...
E put finger prints because hand e put it.
Where you grab it thing, you know.
Fruit or cutting it anykind...with your fingers!
They put it finger prints.
They said...
        "They can look."

Some foot prints...
That's the one they feel it.
They used to feel it turtle there
or might be water-python, snake.
They feel...
        "Hey! Snake!"

That way all that painting they left it behind,
dead...on the rock.

No matter who is.
E can feel it way I feel it in my feeling.
You'll be same too.
You listen my story and you will feel im
because spirit e'll be with you.
You cannot see but e'll be with you and e'll be with me.
This story just listen careful.

Spirit must stay with us. E longside us.
E can feel it spirit e's there.
That way all that dreaming they left...to see.

YOU MUST NOT LOSE

I know some feeling
Feeling like me
But somebody else must listen hard this one

Facing page:
Namarrkon the Thunderman, with stone axes that cause lightning
attached to body; the band surrounding his figure is lightning
- unknown artist, Oenpelli 1955.

White-European they coming now, listen this story
because this story wasn't anyplace.
Other Aborigine somewhere, same story
but they worry about this culture.
This the one...culture, now.

You must not lose, leave your culture behind and story.
You got to hang on and give it behind...your children.
Keep going.

If you got story, heart...
then speak yourself, stand for it!

Man ask you,
        "We want story, before story."

Anybody sit right round.
Listen this man!

He was standing.
What we call Iwarudtj.
One man e standing talking to us. No answer in my day.
I was lying down.
This man with womerra and two spear, standing,
telling story.

So e like this story I follow now.
Telling, telling, telling.
Just listen careful.
One man, that's all.

You got to think about kids behind us.
They got to listen this story
because they might go White-European way.
I don't know what they'll believe.

If they hang on this culture for us, they'll say...
> "Oh, we got culture, we got story,
> we got 'business', we got oh!
> So you stay there, I stay here.
> If you don't want me, well you can stay there
> because I got this."

> "What for?"

> "This one I can't give it to you.
> This one is mine. Another one is yours.
> Because little bit heavy this one
> and that...little bit light.
> I think so, I reckon. Because you coming ask me.
> You know, you ask me anything...
> I'll keep it this one...in my pocket!
> Something like that. Should be.
> No-matter you hard, me hard
> but you must understand this...
> in my culture, in my story, in my Djang
> you got to understand first...after, I give you.
> But if you rush...
> I might be wrong, you might be wrong. I don't know.
> But I might be right, you might be wrong.
> That's it you see."

We...we like story
because story going with your body.
You can listen careful,
when you go sleep you thinking...
        "Oh good story! I like that story.
        I want to keep it."

Feeling...or out of your feeling...your own body.
And you see another man, bit rough man
or might be ten men...they won't listen this story
because they thinking silly.
No-matter who is, no-matter who. This story all same.
You sleep in the night but your body, feeling, there.
While you sleep e working too, with us...yourself.
But other people, no good,
they don't understand I don't think.
But one mistake, little mistake, e might say...
        "Oh, I'm headache. I feel sick, feel funny!"

You feel funny alright
because might be even wrong sleep...
you missing lot this story.
I know Aborigine worse than White-European.
Them people no story. That way they get accident.
I can listen...
        "Accident; e's dead!"

Because e lose this.
Aborigine e would have bin listen this story,
careful...and think!

When you read...
exactly right and you can feel yourself, anyone.
That way I feeling myself putting this story.
You've got to feel.
E don't listen e don't like...well doesn't matter
because you feel something and I feel other.
I feel in my feeling with this story. I think myself...
I don't want to lose this story. I still got im this story.
E can listen careful and how you want to feel.

I know some feeling, feeling like me
but somebody else must listen hard this one.

No good I explain.
If man or woman e don't worry about this story,
just leave im, just let im go.

Man e don't know...
e can make plenty story there but that only silly.
This one with the spirit.

Culture, story...story for anybody, kid, woman.
Must hang on this story and understand.
Listen carefully White-European,
        "What for?"

Because e might feel his body with the blood, water,
feeling. Story good for you.
That way e build this world for us.
That way that story...
We came this world, animal and man and woman.

X-ray mimi spirits - Unknown artist, Oenpelli 1948.

No-matter they go school.
I went school, half of it.
But if they lose...no good.
They can keep im this culture and go school.
They can go school but this story, spirit, dream,
e got to keep im.
E got to keep it this story because this the one.

Story for us, no-matter where...grow up our children.
E'll forget some of them but good for kid.
Got to be keep going.

This story exactly strong.
Want to hang on for ever and ever.
You get children...you teach it!
You teach im, teach im, teach im.
E can pick im up.
E don't know...you teach im!

Frogs - unknown artist, Oenpelli 1948.

In my cousin tribe, on Ulbu side...
his father e was telling story.

Sugarbag - Maningrida 1967.

E was laying down quiet
and other man used to walk away...
"Come back!"

E never come back.
"Come back you two!"

Well one of them used to come back.
Other man...
"Ahh! I don't like that story!"

"This story important,
You got to hang on.
This story for you."

"Ahh! I don't want to listen that."

His brother, e said...
"Come on. We'll listen quiet.
Daddy can tell us."

"No. I don't want to listen to old man."

"Alright, e can go."

No more daytime now. They start laying down.
This old man e telling story.
This young fella don't answer im.
Other one used to go, run away...
"Hey! Come back! Listen to me."

Every night, story...
    "Well I'll tell you story this.
    This one, ahh, special one...
    Mimi, Mimi story.
    Mimi e's a man and very thin.
    That man e go sit in the rock.
    E look..."Oh, my people there".
    E like us. E like anybody.
    E can't kill us but e unkind
    and his trouble...we can't see im!
    But e like you, e like anybody.
    E watching all this secret places.
    E looking after.
    E from rock country.
    Might be few painting in the cave.
    E just draw..."

    "No! I don't want to listen."

The Waramuntjuna, spirit people who
live on a rocky sland at the mouth of the
Liverpool River. They permit the capture
of small turtles, but if large turtles are
taken they create waves which sink
the canoes and drown the hunters.
All are wearing feathered headress,
and one man is making music with
a tube passed through a rock
- unknown artist, Oenpelli 1948.

Little bit story...e run away.

Other fella e was laying down quiet,
watching im old-man telling story.

Other one e say...
    "Ahh...that only silly that!"

His sister...
    "Come on you two woman laying down there."

Same thing.
That two woman used to run away.

Used to tell im story that boy.
Just like school they went...ask, ask.
Little thing...used to tell im.
    "Here! Look that star there."
    "What that?"
    "No! Just look."

Used to look how that night all fine, no cloud.
Well e working on and off that star...
    "See e working?"
    "No!"

"You look!"

"That no good. E can't give me flavour."

"E'll give you.
 E got power.
 While you laying down e'll work.
 Look down that star..."

Own father.
Own daughters had. Own son.
That three they walk away...

"What for you walk away?"

"We don't like im.
 We don't like im hearing you.
 We don't want that story listen."

"This story for you and me.
 I give you story.
 Might be sometime something happen to you.
 Bad, very bad sick,
 You might have sick on your legs, you can't walk
 or might be back, might be head...
 you never know."

"What you...doctor?"

"I not doctor but I just put it through your feeling."

That other fella e listen quietly.

"See that stone there?"

"Yes, I can see."

"Right...that tree you see?"

"Yes, I see tree."

"What over there; see that plain?"

"Yes."

"What e can see?"

"Oh...I can see bird there."

"I see. What about that side; billabong?"

"I see water."

"What else?"

"Oh...lily."

"What e can eat there?"

"Lily!"

"And what you go hunting for in the water?
What you get?"

Sugarbag and diverbird - *Bijinyarra*, Maningrida 1967.

Three Barramundi - Oenpelli 1971.

"Fish."

"What else?"

"Long-neck turtle."

"What else?"

"Oh...might be catfish, file-snake..."

"What that for?"

"Well I feel like to eat!"

"Yes...and what spirit say?"

"I don't know."

Facing page:
The story of the tortoise and the echidna - *Mangudja,* Oenpelli 1968.

"That spirit e tell you to go get im.
You go, you find might be turtle there.
E show you..."There, there!
There's that long-neck turtle."
You find im.
Spirit longside you.
E like that in your eye...you can't look.
Just like nothing...Mimi same."

A billabong where creeks converge. The insects are waterbugs
which the tortoise eats - Maningrida 1971.

"What this one here?"

"This one plum. E can eat im.
E sweet one, good flavour."

"What this climbing here; vine?"

"Oh, that yam."

"What you do?"

"You got to dig im up, get im that yam
and plant it again.
E grow again that yam...that story."

"What this one?"

"Oh that jabiru...sitting down there longa billabong."

"Yes. What for?"

"Well e sitting down something to eat.
E might be hungry."

"What e looking for?"

"Might be little fish, might be frog
or lizard e can eat...before dark e full!"

"I see. What that two there?"

"Brolga."

"What they eat there?"

"Oh...brolga they eat nuts.
Lily nuts, little, little one.
They dig im. They can find im."

"How all this animal they can find im?"

"They know how to find."

"Daddy! We got to go get goose egg.
We don't want to listen that story."

"Alright, e can go. Please yourself. Go get egg."

Two female lizards - Croker Is. 1967.

Morning time...
E said...
>"Come on, I tell you story."

That other boy e said...
>"I go!
>I won't listen to you dad.
>You only telling us liar."

They walk away.
That fella e gone...e never come back!

Other young fella e sleep now...
>"Oh...lovely sleep.
>Hey! Where my brother? Two sister, where?"
>"I don't know. They gone."

That two woman they went there, they find somebody.
Wicked man, short man...his name,
Warrawarrayngumuwar.
That old man e know.
E said...
>"Leave im. It's alright."

This fella e gone...e find crocodile!
So e play round with him.
Might be crocodile bin kill im!

Crocodile and the Milky Way - Yirrakala 1967.

So dark now...

    "Hey! My brother! I better follow."

    "No! You can't go!"

    "What for?"

    "No! You stay!"

    "I can go find im?"

    "No!
    You stay. You believe me.
    If you go you won't come back."

Morning...
E tell im young fella...

    "Alright...you better go looking for."

    "What for?"

    "Go round longa bank and e can look all along river.
    I bet you you look your brother head!"

    "Who tell you?"

    "Just go. Believe me.
    Get barramundi for us."

And that boy e believe im.
E went, e follow bank all the way.
E get one barramundi, two...enough.
E was walking along and e look head there.
E look...

    "My brother!"

Maningrida, 1971.

Crocodile bin kill im.
That head e brought im back.
In the bank e left it.
Crocodile e cutted his neck, e left it high.
So this time crocodile e kill you'n'me.
That head e take im back dry place
because e frightened eye.
E can't look you'n'me eye.
So e took it back there
and all that body e ate it.
That old man e was know!

E was crying all the way...run...
"Daddy you was right, e got im!"

"I told you."

"How about my two sister?

"Might be something they bin find im."

"They won't come back?"

"Yes they'll come back. Might be two, three day."

They come back...
"Ahh...don't look this way, we sick!"

They bin put im down head.
That two woman they bin walk there, sit down...
"Daddy!"

Old man e never answer
because they never listen to him.
"Daddy! E can listen?"

E never answer.
"Hey daddy! Answer us!
Where brother?"

Other one e was laying down.
That young fella didn't want to say because e was shame.

Two days e never answer.
Morning...

    "Daddy! You want to answer us?"

    "What for?"

    "We tell im you story.
    We bin find something there."

    "Yes I know.
    You never listen to me."

    "We alright.
    We bin find im you alright."

    "No! You never listen to me.
    So what for I help you now?
    My feeling...you never listen to me,
    you never help me...I won't help you!
    You're my two daughter alright but I won't.
    You never listen.
    My tongue, my mouth...small
    but you never listen."

Saltwater crocodile in carved wood - Bathurst, Melville Is. 1971.

E told them...
"When e's just about sunset, that sun e go down...
you two be dead!
That thing e kill you two.
Man, that short bloke, Warrawarrayngumuwar,
e kill you two."

Well they never believe im.
That old man e told im, told im...
one man e understand.

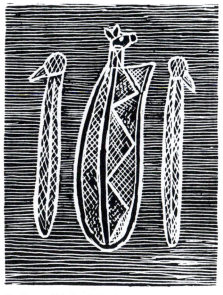

The Mamandi Matjiba Spirits whose sharp hooked spears catch and kill.
Knowing about fire they heat stones on which to cook their victims
- unknown artist, Oenpelli 1948.

"Well daddy, what I go now?"

"I don't know. What you want to go?"

"Out hunting I go. I go bush-honey."

E went there. E get im all that wax, honey.
Oh proper honey everywhere!
E bin come back carrying paperbark...that honey.
They bin eat that day alright...

"Tomorrow what?"

"I don't know. You think about."

"Well I go barramundi."

E went there. Oh e get im barramundi alright.
Next day...

"I go turtle."

Well sometime when we go bush...

"What tomorrow? I go something else."

Sugarbag - Maningrida 1967.

Might be tomorrow might be geese.
Next day you might go file-snake.
Might be other day you might go honey.
No worries that time.

But this time we little bit worry...working.
Balanda e make little bit work, job.
Well not much hunting, only week-end.
That day...no worries.
This time you think about...
      "I don't want to miss that job
       because I get money."

So worry you'n'me.
Don't think about one way...job.
Job no good, money no good...
e only bin come today!
But this the one e done it now old man.

So people e like fishing.
E want a barramundi...because e made that Law.
We follow...everyone.
No-matter white-man, Yellow, Black-man...same.
Me I look...ahh, e got to go fishing but I think...
All same. Same story.
They go fishing because you feel...
      "I want to eat fish.
       I want to eat long-neck turtle
       because that's my tucker."

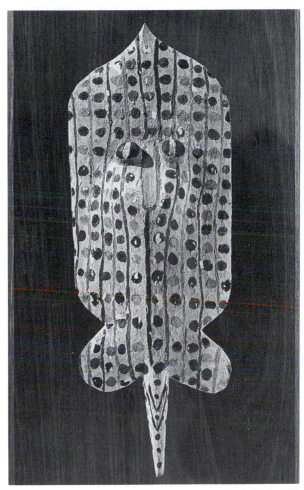

Stingray in painted wood - unknown artist, Croker Is. 1965.

Spirit Man - Oenpelli 1971.

EARTH

And they keep on they asking
That way Aborigine say
"Too much asking."

- unknown artist, Darwin Gallery item 55.

Wak bears a raisin-like fruit with a hot taste.
Food for both man and emu, Ngurrurduh.
The tracks of the emu are there
- *Bunkaniyal*, Maningrida 1979.

Ground...
We hang on.
This earth for us.
Just like mother, father, sister.
Me, I say...
"Just like you'n'me brother or father."

Something under here.
E listen to you. E listen for us.
Might be Rainbow...but e listen.
That way they told me...
"No matter you walking around,
that's the one just like your mother."

"What this road for?
What for big road?"

They want transport from Oenpelli...
bringing store from town.
Came from Murganella...everybody.
Three, four, might be more that six Toyota
We went follow that 'Djidbidjidbi', Mt Brockman road.
Seen it all that bore.
E wasn't bore looking for water, no.
E was looking for that mining.

Oh I ask question; I said...
    "Hey! What under?"
    "Couple a'ton!"
    "Oh!"

I didn't know people was sitting down there,
sitting on this land here and the riches underground.
I didn't know.

They said...
    "That million, million dollar!"
    "Why you dig up?"

Because...
    "We want money."

But money for white-man.
This ground for Aborigine.

That last piece e find it now...
        "This mining now, high ground."

I get heart-crack, you know.
I said...
        "Oh! What for?"

So I never get out of Toyota.
I said...
        "That uranium; we might get sick."
        "Its alright, e can come out."
        "No!"

I stay because uranium is poison.
If you stick on your foot well you get sick.
Anyhow, I stayed.

Well...we said...
        "No! We don't want uranium. Gove e start...enough!
        We don't want it here happen again."

No-matter.
Keep on asking, asking, meeting, keep on asking, asking.
People sick of it now.
They say...
        "Alright."

They agree.

And they keep on they asking.
That way Aborigine say...
        "Too much asking!"

"I went and drew some Mardayin from my own country where there is water.
It is a secret place - women and children are not allowed to see it. There is
a crow there by itself at that billabong, it is not swampy country but rocky and
hilly - the billabong is up in the hills. My spirit goes back to that billabong.
I feel I could draw it now - I have not drawn it before."

Oenpelli 1968.

Now Jabiru done, finished. E went ahead.
Pancon e bin ask, ask...
    "Alright e can go ahead."

And market e can't sell im!

Well e can make money.
E get im from underneath, riches in the ground.
E make million, million might be.
But trouble is...dying quick!
People...big mob they might die because lot of money.

E can make million, million,
thousand and million, million dollars
but something e make there and too early for im to dead.

149

That why you want to hang on country, stand for it.
E come ask...stand, fight!
    "No! E not coming through."

Was to tell im that.
But Jabiru e bin come through and Pancon.
Too late I came...middle of it, just about end.
And I said...
    "No-matter."

E can make money alright, somebody make money
but money no good, not worth it.
But country e stay, e can't move, e can't shift around.
Plenty money alright but you got plenty money...
this world now enough.

E give us something to eat, give us life,
tree, water, grass, yam...
Where the one from underneath?

Should be leave im alone.
That one make you worry.

I don't know what got to be five, six year,
might be twenty year...now make me worry.
Because I think before, when I was young, never worry.
Hunting, come back start sleep,
play around, sleep...no worry.

If you go sleep there and something...
"What's that?
What's that noise going in the sky?"

Well e never go before...sky.
E never listen plane, chopper.
I never listen...and this Toyota came.
Well this time I say...
"Worried day, worry now."

You worry country.
Used to be beautiful, nice green.
But now I just look tree
where that bulldozer pull it out.
Man want road...e can't ask you?

You think about yourself, going back.
You say...
"Yes, what for I want road?
I don't want big one road!"

They might say...
"Bitumen!"

You think now...
"I don't want it. Leave im.
Leave im small road."

"We got big truck coming.
We want im more road."

"No! That's all. Leave im!"

But somebody still coming, asking you,
still asking you what you want to change...
"Hey! You want to change?
Want to change your mind?"

That kind no good. They want to leave im.

You might say...
"I can't change im."

But other one or another one...they don't know feeling.
They might say...
"Hey! We can change im."

They spoil im now. That's why I said...
"You leave im man got culture. E think about it."

You say...
"No! Go away.
If you sit I'll walk, I'll leave you."

If you hard, everybody, everyone of us...
if we fight for country...country e stay way it is.
No-matter they can kill us, run over us, but still fight!
We say...
"You can't run over. You can't kill us
because you can't do it!
No! Too many behind so you can't do it.
We stop you. You can't go through. You won't."

E can't because big mob.

E can stand up and say, "No", easy!

Because you love it this world.
Yes, this country, your country, my country...I love im.
I don't want to lose country, somebody take im.
Make you worry.
If somebody take im your country, you'n'me both get sick.
Because feeling...this country where you brought up
and just like you'n'me mother.
Somebody else doing it wrong...you'n'me feel im.
Anybody, anyone...you'n'me feel.

Lightning Spirit Yowg-Yowg
- *Gubargu,* Maningrida 1971.

Nakundia and Munuratan at Blue Mud Bay. Two fishermen carry their fish, sailing canoe, fishing lines. The spearing of one man, two bodies transfixed with spears, the men responsible for the spearing and the avenging ceremonies - Unknown artist, Yirrakala 1948.

But that man e need plenty money...
e digging alright but e killing himself.
Killing his body where e digging.
Killing his granny or grandpa...no-matter e white!
E want badly that money but e killing it himself.
Killing us.

E think about little bit another thing
but that mean e'll get punish.
That spirit e do something.
Might be im burn his house...easy!
Or e might blow up car, e might puncture, anykind.
Because not you'n'me, you'n'me can't because spirit.

Because this story and spirit e watching what e doing.
That spirit e say...
    "Don't do it!
     You do it but might be something happen."

Watching you, watching me.

Spirit e watching him. E say...
    "You can't do it that."

E just put im through his body. E say...
    "Don't do that. Don't do that.
     Don't feel it that. Don't used to it. Leave it.
     Don't interfere with that. Feel im on my side."

155

Dreaming said...
"Don't touch me. Leave me alone."

First Woman she said...
"Don't touch."

Never touch anything and spoil country.
Would have bin stay like used to be
and people should feel better.
"Well we supposed to dig close to Mt Brockman."

But we said...
"No!
Might be no good for you.
Don't touch this one. Leave it.
Better go back about three mile, four mile.
You do it there is good."

Is not bad...only King Brown dream, King Brown dreaming.
I think they dig...they'll find it that mother one.
You know, 'way e starting'.
That mining e spread out but they'll find middle of it.
Well that dreaming!

We fright water.
That Woman done it.
E seen it, e said...
"Ahh...new fresh water e got to come down."

Of course...because everybody we drinking.
You drinking because give us life.
If something, that digging, mine business,
if that water e'll crawl through there,
e'll destroy our plants,
tree, fish and might be people.
I reckon our people might be first.
That way I bit fright or scared.

Because changing it I feel.
You can't see change because this country nice country,
nice enough for anybody to look at.
Because we came that country for made.
We came with it, bird and we, animal and we.

Plain...
Flood plain they call it now
but plain for anybody, no-matter who.
But something in water there, something to eat.
Your food all in that water.
Long-neck turtle, lily, file-snake, fish, catfish...
good to eat, in that billabong.
If that something e come in that water,
what happen if no fish, no lily?
We can't eat any!
If we eat one or two we sick eh!
What about before?
Now I'm scared little bit
because they used to drink before, oh anywhere.
This time bit fright now.

Because this riches,
riches place in the ground, under this ground
but e kill our blood and body.

E might go find something, e'll find.
E dig, e might find im...not yellow something,
mining, uranium e find it...but something else.
Because e humbug.
E shouldn't be humbug the ground we sitting on.
We sitting on for us.
Not for me, yourself or somebody else, no...for world.
Everybody...bird, dog, dingo, buffalo, horses and man.

Spirit people dancing on mountain top - Oenpelli 1967.

Anyhow, that one here last year, but e went ahead.
E didn't worry about.
And I said...
        "I don't know about twenty years' time.
        This land got to be change
        because e would have bin stay like way e was,
        before...should be."

Because that story went through.
E left each clan and e would have bin stay.

And now half the ground e take; White-European.
Spoiling it. E take it half of our culture doing that mining.
Not fair because Aborigine can't do anything about.
E can't take White-European country half of it
because no good.
I don't think so Aborigine can do because bit fright.
Another country e can't. E got to stay where e belong to.

E'll be dead. So Aborigine e say...
        "Well behind our children.
        They'll carry on this culture, 'business',
        secret, Djang and that Ring-place."

Children...we say...
        "You hang on this tight!"

I don't know twenty years time, forty years might be.
They might come in close.
Now is close to us. We got to watch im.
E came through alright. E came...e got im.
I don't know twenty years I thinking myself.

So I said...

"This culture you got to hang on
and you hang on piece of ground for you."

I'm telling these kids because I'll be dead.

"You got to be bit tough. Don't be fright."

I'm telling my son...

"Don't go round and put your head down.
If you want to speak that man,
go and speak to that man.
If you fright you won't say.
I'll be dead...you won't be speaking.
This man e'll come in close to you.
So now get hit off me and say something!

I not growl you. I can growl you alright.
I can hit you if I want to
but you got to hang on this one.
I can hit you with this stick, with this culture
because you got to get this
and you'll be the tough man if you want to.

Now give you heart-crack or strongly word
so you hang on this culture.
Don't forget."

I said...

"When you sleep, you think...
they want you work there, money and friendly.
Yes, you friendly but you think this, this story.
You hang on same thing like I'm doing.
I can go, run around but I still got im
in my back, in my front because heart.

This ground, tree, water, anything...for us.
Body in your body.
You cover, you sleep, you sleep with earth.
Earth for us, lily, any sort of a thing, plum.
This Toyota not for us but we learning something.
But e don't want to forget.
I don't forget."

"What's wrong with Toyota?"

I said...

"Well something wrong!"

I had a argue little bit but I hang on my culture.

Diver bird, painted wood - Oenpelli 1968.

Oenpelli 1971.

162

WE LIKE WHITE-MAN ALL RIGHT

We like white-man alright
We like im city
But city make you sick of it
Better this

Where they say we rich.
Yes, we rich alright...not really!
Aborigine e rich man e got change clothes, clean clothes,
look pretty-boy, yes.
But me I think...
Aborigine had chain in the neck first go!

First Aborigine e saw it white-Man...
e put it people, chain longa neck
because they pinch it cattle.
They shouldn't.
They get police...e put chain.
Now...court they take im in but before...chain.

Wild, wild people.
They never see white-man.
They said...
        "They might run away.
         We can't catch im. Too many bushes."

So they put chain.

But wasn't Aborigine fault.
White-European didn't make friend with Aborigine.
That first go e put chain!

But what about White-European they coming in this
world?
What about that chain in the leg?
They row...long chain everyone of them.
Same thing. They was prisoner too!

Before they came this everyone bin have im chain.
Now all bin settle now...settle down.

Should be missionaries first they started
and asking people this culture.
What they done?
They run it quick!

They brought in something too...drinking.
Before, they should first ask question
about dreaming, story, cave, people.
They bin rush in.
They took up school...teach.
Now Aborigine losing it now.
They lose it already, I know,
I guess that.
And they running drinking.
They should be keep for a while...after.
No...they was too quick.
So wasn't Aborigine fault...White-European fault.

That missionary e telling Bible there...
         "Oh you got to remember up there
          and you got to be become good."

Same thing Aborigine if lot of story.
I used to go church but I hang on this.
Because I can't say liar...e's true.
E's very true this story.

Diver bird, painted wood - Oenpelli 1968.

We know White-European got different story.
But our story, everything dream,
dreaming, secret, 'business'...
you can't lose im.
This story you got to hang on for you,
children, new children, no-matter new generation
and how much new generation.
You got to hang on this old story because the earth,
this ground, earth where you brought up,
this earth e grow, you growing little by little,
tree growing with you too, grass...

I speaking story
and this story you got to hang on, no matter who you,
no-matter what country you.
You got to understand...this world for us.
We came for this world.

We say we don't like each other.
Ahh...no good we don't like each other. What for?
E not from somewhere else!

That why you stand for it.
No-matter who different, different country...
all same thing.

We like white-man alright. We like im city
but city make you sick of it. Better this...
no-matter little house, little road
and others where no road,
e can see something there, green, tree...

Now e's lovely over there.
E's feeling now...wind...e coming.
Now we telling story e start blow.
E pumping now that leaf, that blood there.
E not wood but you'n'me that.
E man but e listen for you'n'me. E listen.

Yesterday I feel it because I was tired
and last night...oh, I feel it terrible, I nearly dead.
Because I never come put im this story.
I feel it yesterday afternoon too...no wind...no story!
Today e feeling now.
That wind e love, love, love.
I love wind.
E blowing...nice country in the plain.

E can blow.
Star...e can look.
All the same, all same.
You can't change it.
That world e was like that now.

Rumuk, the scrub fowl. Rumuk eats the flowers of
Karndawalk, Coral tree - *Bunkaniyal,* Maningrida 1979.

This Law, country, people...
no-matter who you people,
red, yellow, black and white...
but the blood is same.
Country, you in other place
but exactly blood, bone...e same.

And all my people all dead
but we got few, that's all.
Not much, not many...getting too old
and young-fellas I don't know they hang on this story.

All my uncle gone
but this story I got im.
They told me, taught me
and I can feeling.
Feeling with my blood or body,
feeling all this tree and country.
While you sitting down e blow,
you feel it wind
and same this country you can look
but feeling make you.

Feeling make you out there with wind, open place
because e coming through your body
because you're like that.
Have a look while e blow, tree
and you feeling with your body
because tree just about like your brother or father
and tree watching you.

Flying foxes - unknown artist, Darwin Gallery item 54.

Someone can't tell you.
Story e telling you yourself.
E tell you how you feel because tree or earth
because you brought up with this earth,
tree, eating, water.

That way they give us talk.

So I'm saying now,
earth is my mother or my father.
I'll come to earth.
I got to go same earth
and I'm sitting on this dirt is mine
and children they playing.
Tree is mine.
In my body that tree.

This story I'm telling it
because I was keeping secret myself.
I was keeping in my mind with the culture
and see other people what they was doing
and I was feeling sad you know.
White-European different story
what we new generation now,
different story.
Because school doing it and something else
and our people they forget that.
They going little by little.

They shouldn't be, they not supposed to,
should be the man with the pressure...
put it on this.
No-matter about that White-European,
e can go with that one
but must White-European got to be listen this culture
and this story
because important one this.

This on my Bunitj Clan I put it.

Yam stick, Uwar rituals, Croker Is. 1967.

Ubirr in the Northern

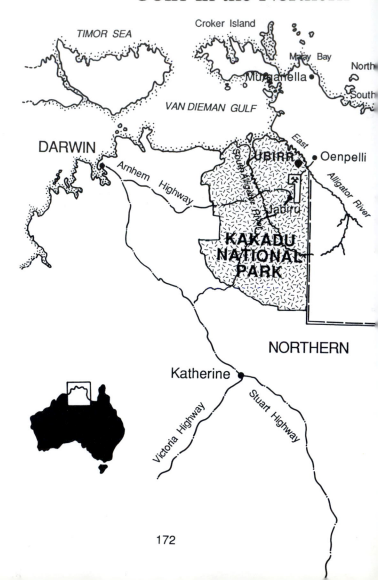

Territory of Australia

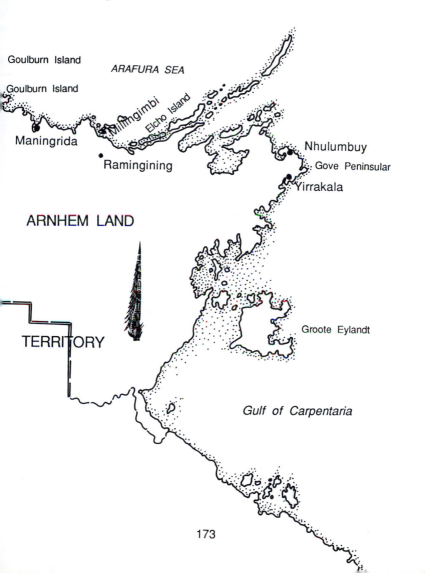

Goulburn Island

ARAFURA SEA

Goulburn Island

Maningrida

Milingimbi

Elcho Island

Ramingining

Nhulumbuy

Gove Peninsular

Yirrakala

ARNHEM LAND

TERRITORY

Groote Eylandt

Gulf of Carpentaria

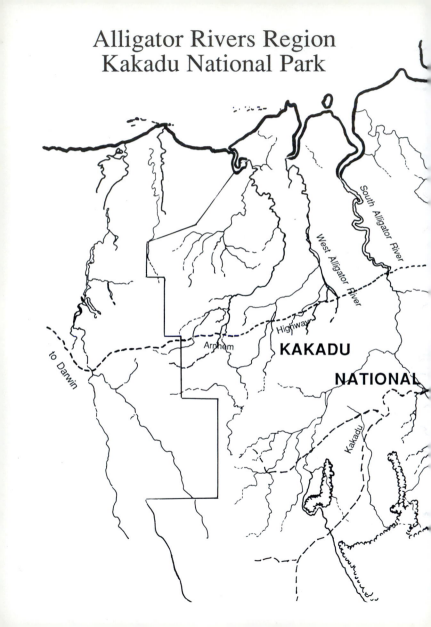

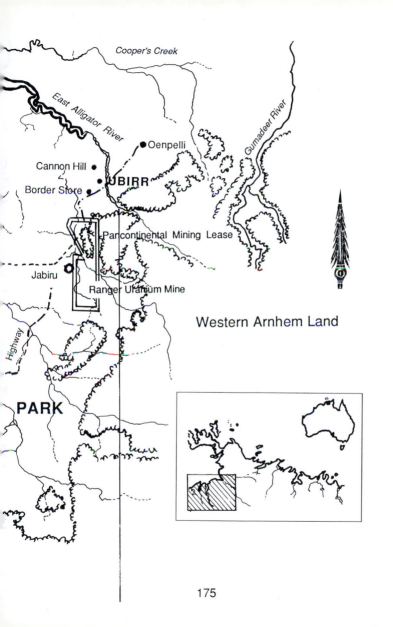

Cooper's Creek

East Alligator River

Gumadeer River

●Oenpelli

Cannon Hill ●

Border Store ● ● **UBIRR**

Pancontinental Mining Lease

Jabiru

Ranger Uranium Mine

Western Arnhem Land

Highway

PARK

GLOSSARY

Adanggadang	a clan group of the Iwadja tribe
Amurdak	a tribe of people
Anykind	anything, any sort of thing, any way
Arnhem Land	see maps, pp 172-5
Badbanarrwarr	Jabiru
Balanda	White person, white-European
Bandicoot	insectivorous and herbivourous marsupial
Barramundi	a large freshwater fish
Barra	Barramundi
Billabong	wetland pool or water-hole, often perennial
Brolga	large bird of the crane species
Bukurnidja	a tribe of people
Bunitj	Bill Neidjie's clan group
Croker	Croker Island, see maps pp 172-5
Cupside	to tip out or over, e.g. to tip out of a cup
Dhuwa	social grouping, one of two parts; moiety
Didgeridoo	a large wood-wind instrument
Djang	sacred power emanating from the Dreaming
Djidbidjidbi	Mt Brockman
E; e	he, she or it
Elcho	Elcho Island, see maps pp 172-5
E'll; e'll	he, she or it will
E's; e's	he, she or it is
Gagudju	a language group; (Kakadu)
Gadurra	a clan group of the Iwadja tribe
Goanna	large monitor lizard
Gove	peninsula, see maps pp172-5
Gulluban	flying-fox
Gunmurrgurrgurr	the term for a clan group
Gunwandul	first lightning
Im; im	him, her or it
Imself; imself	himself, herself or its self
Indjuwanydjuwa	ancestral being

Irwardbad Iwarudtj	King-Brown snake (Yirrbardbarrd) story
Jabiru	town; see maps pp 172-5 bird; large stork
King Brown Kunapipi	large venomous snake,Pseudechis Australis creation, rebirth ceremony
Longa Longside	belonging to; in; alongside; beside
Manganawal Mbukarla Mia mia Murganella	a tribe of people a tribe of people large body-sores small settlement, see map page 172-3
Oenpelli Oobarr	town, see maps pp172-5 'business'
Pancon Paperbark	Pancontinental Mining Company tree; bark from a paperbark tree
Ranger-mine	Ranger Uranium mine
Stringybark-canoe	made from bark of stringybark tree
Turn	to become, to turn into
Ubirr Ulbu	sacred place, see maps pp172-5 a clan group of the Amurdak tribe
Warramurrauung Warrgarr Wet Womerra	mother of Gagudju people flying fox food the wet-season of heavy monsoonal rains spear throwing tool
Yirridtja Yiwurrum You'n'me Young-fella(s)	social grouping, one of two parts; a moiety a language group (also Ikurrumu) you and me young men

STORY LIST

Artists' brushes - W.A Art Gallery Aboriginal Collection.

The bark paintings and artifacts reproduced in this book came mainly from Oenpelli, Maningrida and Croker Island, with smaller numbers from Millingimbi, Ramingining, Elcho and Groote Eylandt. These are all locations on or adjacent to the far north coast of Australia in the region of the Northern Territory.

Thanks to the artists and families of those communities. The bark paintings, some collected as long ago as 1948, are held in the collections of the West Australian Art Gallery, Perth, West Aust., and the Northern Territory Museum and Art Gallery, Darwin, N.T.

The painters of some of these works have died. In those cases the name of the artist cannot be displayed since it is the custom to no longer speak of them by name. These paintings are ascribed to the communities from which they came.